QUESTIONS FOR GOD?

Compiled, Edited, and Illustrated by
David Liverett

Other books by David Liverett:

When Hope Shines Through

Faith for the Journey

Love, Bridges of Reconciliation

Light from the Barn
A collection of stories and art reflecting country life

This Is My Story
146 of the World's Greatest Gospel Singers

They Called Him Sparky
Friends' Reminiscences of Charles Schulz

Just Beyond the Passage
Life's Changes in Art and Story

Those Grand Ole Country Music Stars

Oh, to be in Miss Collier's class again!
Christie Smith Stephens and David Liverett

Chinaberry House

Production assistance: Combustoica
WWW.COMBUSTOICA.COM

Copyright © 2009 by David Liverett
December 2009
All rights reserved.
For permission to reproduce any part or form of the text, or artwork contact the publisher.

ISBN 978-0-578-04680-8

Dedication

This book is dedicated in memory of
Charles Nelson Moore, pastor, counselor,
and mentor to me during a tumultuous
period in my life. It was the early 1960s and
I was still in my teens, when Charles Moore
saw potential in my life as I struggled with
my own questions of God. I owe much to
his caring and loving ministry.

Injustice

I rant.
I rave.

Sister of Job,
I shake my fists
at the heavens,
scream into the night.

Such suffering.
Such pain.

Where are you?
Where are you?

Can you not help?
Send the rowboat?
Send the helicopter?

And then I hear the question,
the question to me from
the Author of All Life,

What are you doing,
what are you doing
with that pen I placed
in your hand?

Christie Smith Stephens
February 14, 2006

Introduction

Ronald V. Duncan

The value of faith in the twenty-first century is being questioned, tested, and tried as never before. With the explosion of knowledge and the awareness of the world, men and women are being bombarded with questions and situations requiring attentiveness, due diligence, deliberation, wisdom, and courage. The paradigms of the past may not suffice to answer adequately the problems of the present—or the future. So what is being called for in this present time?

Collaboration of the saints is of paramount importance in our current milieu. We have as a nation, endured twenty plus years of individualism and egomania running rampant. The results of such behavior have created confusion, chaos, and lack of commitment to values that sustain and strengthen our society. The emerging generation is calling for our culture to be authentic, engaged in community, and seeking answers that make a difference in the lives of people. So what does collaboration of the saints look like?

The church has a wonderful opportunity to address the pressing questions, problems, and issues with confidence, as we are led by the Holy Spirit. The church should be leading the charge by providing forums for discussion, participating in blogs, engaging in meaningful dialogues, and challenging one another to a deeper walk with God. God is not afraid of our questions, but we may be afraid to ask them. Asking difficult questions with a pure motive is a sure step for positive growth in our lives. Ignorance is what feeds paranoia and ineffective solutions. So what can I do?

Each one of us can engage one another in a supportive environment of learning and growing together. Our questions should bind us together rather than alienate our relationships. This means we reframe the meaning of questions as a positive step of growth. Understanding one's self is certainly among the foundational blocks needed for meaningful engagement. When it comes to asking God questions, we must be open to the reverse—God's questions for us.

The intent of this book is to provide opportunity to ask questions: questions that will stretch us; questions that will strengthen us; questions that will sustain us as we deal with life. Use this resource in small groups, classes, and conversa-tions. It can lead you to a deeper relationship with God. As you travel the path of growing in grace, be sure to walk with others who may shed light on your path.

Foreword

Mort Crim

The title of this book is short and simple. But it embraces the most complex and difficult theme ever to challenge the human mind. That theme can be stated in one word:

Why?

Why is there anything instead of nothing?

Why does evil exist?

Why is there suffering?

Why am I here?

In the following thought provoking pages, you will encounter other questions including, no doubt, some of your own.

The questions are not unique. People have been asking them since the dawn of time and for nearly as long, theologians, philosophers, and scientists have been attempting to find satisfying answers.

Some of the questions on the following pages simply can never be answered. Philosophers can formulate theories about the nature of reality, scientists can add to our knowledge of *how* things work, theologians and religious teachers can define God both in abstract, theoretical ways and in terms of experience. But even the most brilliant minds are quite incapable of answering the biggest *why* questions.

And so to pose questions to God is to articulate something we know cannot be answered because we are presenting the questions to a being, a presence, a mystery, an *ultimate* which by definition is beyond our understanding.

What, then, is the value of drafting questions that can't be answered to a *God* who can't be fathomed?

Perhaps the value is in the process itself.

Reading how others have phrased the questions, how they have struggled with them, how by faith they have transcended them, may help you on your own pilgrimage.

The questions can so overwhelm us that we may conclude there's just no point in asking them.

The writers of these chapters would vigorously disagree. While their questions may reflect the uniqueness of their own life's experiences, there is a cohesiveness to this book that can be expressed in a single word: *faith*.

In these pages you will encounter a faith that bridges across unanswerable questions to a relationship beyond question.

You will feel the agony and pain of believers who've struggled mightily with life's biggest questions without be-coming cynical or despairing; who think if Jesus himself once cried out, "My God, why have you forsaken me?" then it's no betrayal of faith to have their own questions for God.

The problem with the questions has little to do with the questions. The problem is that we often try to answer the questions alone. The reflections and stories in this book are good places to begin that dialogue with others who have asked them already and are living into the answers. But there is a need greater than personal reflection through a book: join with others. Use this book as a core for a small guest group. You can be certain that nearly everyone, at one time or another, has these kinds of questions. In a Sunday school class, a small group, even with your family, the stories of these fellow travelers can help you to work your way through to a good and faithful answer for your own journey.

Preface

I have so many questions about life. Some of my questions are very mundane and I have decided that I can Google some of the answers. As I am writing this on December 7, 2009, I am very much aware that three years ago, on this date, I was told that I had cancer. Last week I was told that it has now spread to my right leg which makes walking difficult.

David and his grandfather,
E. L. McConnell, 1945

Starting radiation today gives me some hope that I will be able to walk down the aisle at my son's wedding in four months.

My journey with cancer and two stories of my own life may explain why I have chosen to develop this book. When I was sixteen months old, my grandfather bought a burial insurance policy on me. I had whooping cough and had been struggling to breathe for hours. My family thought it was just a matter of time before I would succumb to one of the most deadly diseases that especially affected infants in the 1930s and 1940s. Apparently, God had a different plan for my life.

Growing up in the church has given me plenty of "simple" answers to questions I still encounter daily. Dealing with an incurable cancer certainly brings out questions. My daily prayer, since my stem cell transplantation two years ago has been: "God loves me and has a plan for my life." Those "simple answers" made the difference in my life. It makes me a very humble person when seventy of my Sunday school class members gather around to pray for me.

A thought came to me this summer: "When life throws you a curve"...*you need a big mitt*. My big mitt is made up of my family and friends who are praying for me. Living a life of hope and faith, I know God can take care of the enormous questions. I still believe in divine healing and living in God's plan. I am contented with these sixty-six years with a wonderful family and friends.

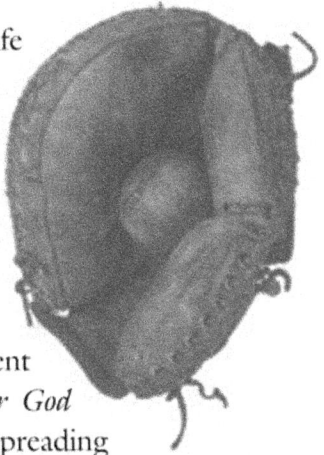

My friends have once again provided the content of this book. The plan was to have *Questions for God* released in December 2009. With the myeloma spreading to my right leg, the date of release has been pushed back to the fall of 2010. There are over eighty writers and entries in this book with a drawing of each contributor. Although many took the theme of telling God how blessed they had been, others took the position of asking God the hard questions of life.

The idea of this book came to me while having my stem cell transplantation in October 2007. The book is meant to be used as a thought starter for small groups. There are several themes that could be discussed. I hope your life can be enriched while reading this collection of *Questions for God*.

David Liverett
Anderson, Indiana
December 7, 2009

———————————∞———————————

An interesting note: Three of the contributors for this book have now had the opportunity to receive their answers from the Almighty as they have passed away —Gene Newberry, Charles Moore, and Barry Hoffman.

Table of Contents

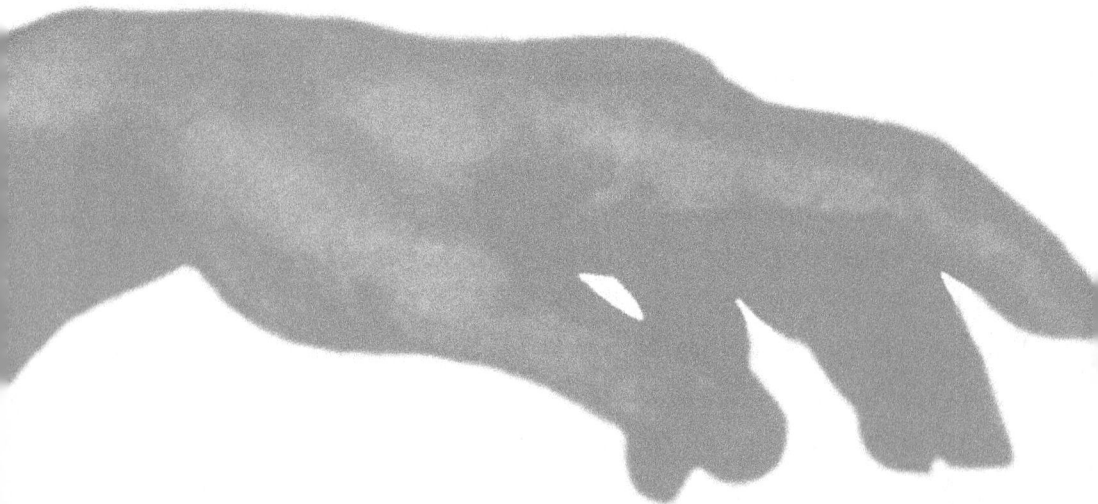

Why Me? Why???

Stephen Hill

D o I have questions for God? Sure, who doesn't? I have a lot of them. I admit some of my questions are small. Some address larger issues. I feel they are all important.

This is only a partial list.

My questions are many and due to a very inquisitive nature. Here goes, why do I ask so many questions? Why is the seed so big in an avocado? How does Moses feel about not getting into the Promised Land? Is the grass really greener on the other side of the fence? Why is time shorter as I get older? For that matter, why am I shorter as I get older? Why do we measure in feet and not hands, except for horses; which don't have hands and only feet? Why does everybody on TV know Your true heart and intentions, when You gave us a handbook in Your own words? Why is the water chestnut the only food that never changes texture no matter how it is prepared? Did my childhood dog make it into heaven and will I get him back? Why are there so many denominations that profess to possess the Truth? How can You love all of us when we are so unlovable? Why is it that Jesus spoke very plainly about loving You and each other and we still can't accept that it is that simple? Does Adam get teased up there, for using Eve as an excuse with the apple? If I did that, I know my buddies would never let me live that one down. Can You really make a mountain out of a molehill? I've heard that expression all my life and still wonder about it. I think we, (humankind), do that a lot (wonder and make mountains, you know).

Why is that? Okay, just one more, Lord, where does that missing sock go? Wait, one more, this is it. I promise....Why me? Why???

Dare We Ask God Anything!

Barry L. Callen

Life in this troubled world encourages questions directed God's way. However, none of them will be asked here. I pose the big issues that should come before any questions.

Ask God questions? What are we assuming about God? Does God hear, care, and answer? If so, dare we mere humans ask questions that throw doubt on the wisdom of God's past actions or apparent present inaction in any circumstance? Who are we to ask anything, try to get information, change a divine intention, share in God's decision-making? Asking is a form of prayer, a conversation with God. Would God pay attention and actually talk to ordinary people? Are we willing to accept as true the Bible's witness to God's being, character, and way of relating to creation—including us? Here are the really big issues.

What is the Bible's witness? These are the highlights. God places the divine self in intimate relationship with the creation. God chooses to be involved in the pain of our human situations of loneliness, sin, sickness, war, and death—and it hurts the Divine deeply that any of these even exist. Yes, God "hurts" too! God plans, but does not manipulate all of the world's details, does not insist on total control of all things at all times. Divine "election" is real, but a voluntary action intended to bring opportunity and hope to us, but without erasing our freedom or accountability. The divine project in this world is all about *restoring right relationships.*

God can and sometimes does "change His mind" in response to changing human attitudes, actions, and prayers, although God's character and purposes never change. Such sensitivity and adjusting is the way of love. God is not threatened by questions—even questions about whether there is a God or why there is evil. Questions are part of a loving relationship between an unlimited God and very limited humans. Prayers, even ones full of questions, are actually encouraged by God—and they can make a difference in the lives of people, and in the life of God. The Bible says and illustrates all of this repeatedly.

So, ask God whatever you will. Be warned, however. If you want to manipulate God for your own agenda, forget it. God is God! But if you are crying out in repentance and love, seeking the highest good of others, and wanting to be made more like Christ and better able to serve, then God says to you, "Bring on your questions!"

Why Me?

Mort Crim

ad things do happen to good people and the first question we tend to ask is, "Why?" If someone we love is struck down by a tragic accident or a terminal illness, our natural response is, "Why her? Why him?"

If it happens to us, personally, we wonder, "Why me?" All of us experience difficulties and sadness for which there is no rational explanation. During my seventy-four years on this earth, I've certainly encountered a fair share.

But there's another "why me" question that has always troubled me and it concerns the wonderful blessings in my life. In a world where most people go to bed hungry and millions die every year from starvation and disease, I would ask God why I was so privileged to arrive in this land of abundance?

Why me?

With so many babies born into situations where they are not wanted and not cared for, why did I grow up in a safe and loving home?

Why me?

In a world where millions long for nothing more than clean, running water, enough food to survive, and a safe, dry place to sleep, why have I been able to take for granted all these basics of existence—and so much more! How is it that I can speak my mind, freely, without fear of jail or torture? Why am I privileged to attend any place of worship I choose—or decide to attend none—with no fear of reprisal?

Why me?

People in many parts of the world live in terror, never knowing when they or their children might be taken away, raped, tortured, shot, or blown up on their way to work or at the market. For millions life is a living hell. Yet I can sleep soundly at night, never worrying about such threats.

Why me?

Applying the "why me" question to the positive events in my life has helped me develop a healthier perspective and permitted gratitude to fill in the places where anger and bitterness might have taken hold. Perhaps the question is just another way of stating what philosophers and theologians have grappled with for centuries: Why is there evil in the world? I believe the companion question has to be: Why is there good in the world?

As I reflect on the wonderful life I've enjoyed, for all it's difficulties and sadness, I certainly would want to ask God why my life has been filled with so much that's good? Why me?

Hello Father God,

Barbara Clausen Theodore

For over fifty years, I have had a question for You regarding divine healing. As you know, my first husband and both of my children died from Huntington's Disease after years of deterioration of body and mind. This was a disease that needed a divine touch. There was no medical help. We had two beautiful, intelligent children. Both accepted Jesus as Lord of their lives and were baptized at a young age. I gave a testimony in our church saying: "How blest we are. We are in the Lord's work. We have a perfect family with a girl and boy. Life could not be better." In less than ten years our world collapsed.

Silent symptoms began in Paul and he was diagnosed at age thirty-three. He lived to be fifty-eight. Countless prayers and many anointings were offered. In two instances, entire congregations gathered around the altars of the church praying for a divine healing. The children and I expected to open our eyes to see Paul jumping to his feet to sing! It did not happen. After years of deepening depression, Paul entered a state hospital because he was a danger to himself and family. Although a profound spirit healing happened, the physical condition continued to deteriorate. In 1987 I had three family members with HD. Paul died in March of that year.

When I saw similar symptoms in David and later in Karen, I could not believe it. This insidious disease was destroying my entire family. So many prayers continued for them and my constant prayer was: "I love them so much but I know You love them even more. Please release them from this prison of disease." David died at age thirty-six after eighteen years of HD and Karen died at age forty-nine after sixteen years. All of their hopes and dreams were shattered. The prayers for divine healing were never answered—not for even one. Although my faith was severely tried, I never lost sight of You. You were my song in the night—You bore me up and gave me rest.

Father God, You gave each of us courage, strength, and grace for each day and supplied all of our needs in countless ways, except this one endless plea. Faith the size of a mustard seed??? We had it!! I did not understand this but finally learned to leave it in Your hands and some day, ask You face to face. Here I am on bended knee. I am listening.

Your devoted daughter,

Just One Question?

Thomas R. Harbon

A question for God—just *one* question. A hundred questions would be easy; ten would be difficult, but just *one* is daunting. His creation staggers the mind with its scope and magnitude. Mankind exists on one tiny planet orbiting a minor star on the edge of a galaxy of billions of stars. And that galaxy is similar to millions of others scattered across the universe. Mankind has existed for only a millionth of the life of the universe. The fraction of His creation that we can see in time and space is an infinitesimal sliver of the whole. What else, who else, is out there? What preceded mankind and what will follow? That's one question I'd like to ask God.

God created heaven and earth and saw that it was good. He put us here to...what? Why are we here? Perhaps to learn about Him; most certainly to choose whether or not to follow Him, to obey Him, to be His children. I'd like to ask Him why we are here.

Then there is the matter of what seems like needless, even pointless suffering of good people. We have all known loved ones, children of God, faithful saints, whose failing bodies have brought them months and years of agonizing pain. Pain that has torn at their minds relentlessly stripped away their feeling, until they are able to do no more than suffer and hope for a quick and merciful end. What purpose does it serve? Why do they have to suffer so? I'd like to ask Him about that.

There are about six billion people alive on earth at this moment. That is a small fraction of the hundreds of billions who have already lived and died. There likely will be even more billions or trillions yet to come, and Earth is one tiny planet in one slice of time in God's vast universe. In spite of these numbers, He knows each of us and calls us by name. He walks with us and talks with us. He even notes the fall of the sparrow and reminds us that we are worth much more than a sparrow.

So if I have just one question for God, I would ask with King David "What is man that thou art mindful of him, and the son of man that thou dost care for him?" With this vast universe to watch over, through all the eons of time, past, present, and future, how is it that You are able, have the interest to know and love *each* of us intimately, to lead us by still waters, to make straight our paths, to send Your Son to die for us that we might live eternally?

If I could ask God one question, that is what I'd ask...because it's too wonderful to comprehend.

Light and Dark

Sara Cook

How can human beings be capable of acts of both extreme humanity and inhumanity? God, what I have witnessed through my work in Northern Ireland has alternately renewed my faith in the generosity of the human spirit and made me realize the extent to which people are able to violate the dignity of others. How is it possible for a person to torture or kill and still be a devoted parent or spouse? If we are made in Your image, how can we have such a deep capacity for brutality?

Just this week I heard a former member of a paramilitary organization and a man who lost his wife to a paramilitary bomb question whether their respective connection to the conflict was an "accident of birth." Sometimes I think that such a question is as close as I can come to making sense of the fact that—through often small twists of fate—some people travel a path that leads to violence. Surely we all have the capacity for violence and brutality. Most of us who lead comfortable, middle-class lives exonerate ourselves from the thought that we too might be capable of acting in ways that counteract Your image in us. Having met people who are funny, warm, engaging, and human...and who have also taken the lives of others drives me to understand that part of myself which might also act in the most inhuman of ways. Does life consist primarily of "therefore by the grace of God go I"?

And what do we do with these contradictions in ourselves and in our societies...these strange mixtures of light and dark? Do we try to understand the push-pull factors that drive violence and inhumanity within ourselves and on local and global scales? Or, do we simply leave the affairs of the world to You and avoid the great weight of worry about the dark side of humanity? At present, I have chosen to live with this increasingly unsettling feeling of realizing that the bomber or gunman or unjust agent of the State could be me. I have also chosen to celebrate the incredible humanity that I witness everyday—the small gestures of reconciliation between former enemies, the unexpected offer of forgiveness, the acknowledgement of the lived experience of "the Other."

God grant us the wisdom to understand the coexistence of humanity and inhumanity and to seek a path that leads to the far side of revenge.

Belief vs. Unbelief

Donald G. Boggs

*G*od, today I once again wondered if You really exist.
I doubted.
    Why is it so hard? Why can't I be certain 24/7/365 in something as fundamental as Your very existence?

Some days I know for certain. When a pregnant Tamara was carrying our daughter Hannah, we found ourselves in Columbus, Ohio, on Good Friday and discovered Tamara was bleeding.

Significantly.

At a Catholic hospital, a sonogram and a doctor's words informed us that the placenta had separated and that the child would quickly be lost. On Easter Sunday, I drove a still pregnant Tamara home. A doctor's visit the next day showed only the most minor problem. We were told we must have misunderstood the doctor's words. We knew better, and after Hannah was born, we sent a photo to the doctor, who wrote that he still remembered. It took a miracle, but...

I believed.

Time went by; challenges came; the mundane overcame the miraculous. The moment lost its immediate power and in the midst of heartbreaking headlines and personal loss, on a given day...

I doubted.

A few years later, I found myself in a waiting room with my pastor during Tamara's exploratory surgery for a likely cancer. I observed the pattern—a surgeon came to the family waiting, but at the door, Tamara's doctor motioned me to come to her and meet with her in private. My imagination went into overtime. This was not the way good news was delivered.

The first words of that highly respected surgeon were "The Lord has healed her." At first I could not even believe this professional who knows so much more about medicine and science than I ever will. But with her assurance and further explanation, I believed not only in Tamara's healing, but in You.

I knew for certain.

Still, though I remember vividly the details of that encounter, my faith still falters. I feel You have been overly generous to me with miracles, knowing that though I find faith in You with the coming of the bluebirds each spring and a variety of daily miracles, sometimes...

I still doubt.

As the father of the demon possessed child spoke to the Christ: *Lord, I believe; help thou mine unbelief* —Mark 9:24 KJV.

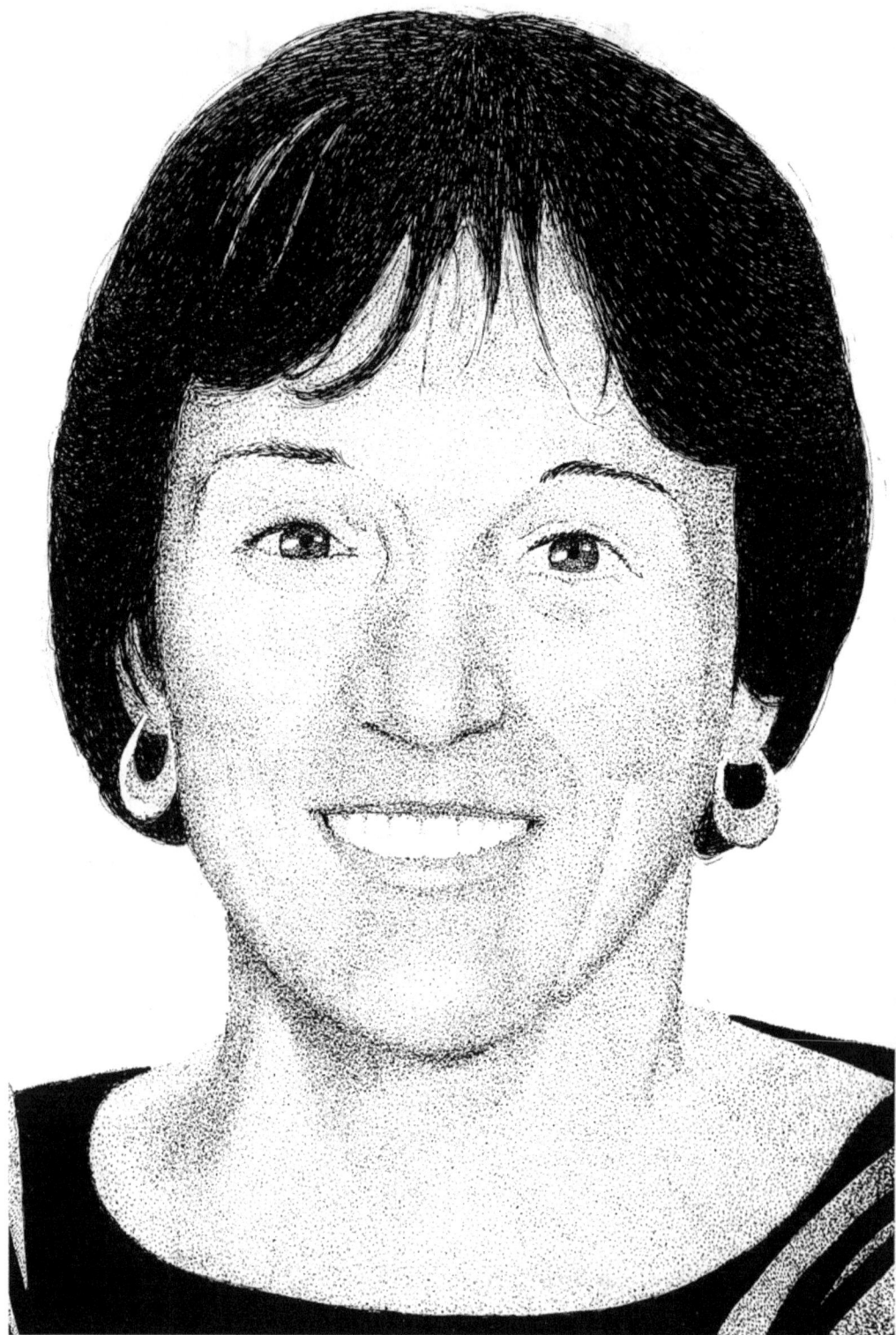

Why?

Cheryl Johnson Barton

*P*erhaps I should have been named Thomas—except for being female. The famous doubter and I certainly are kindred spirits, which is why it's challenging to think of only one question for God. But with thirty years of ministry in Japan, I've zeroed in on this: Why Japan, and why this long? (I just couldn't ask a single question.)

Truthfully, I'm much more drawn to the rhythms of Africa, the flowing scarves and blousy pants of India, the cuisine of China. I love wide-open spaces, yet live in a cramped megalopolis of twenty-seven million people. On top of this, converts to Christ come by the easy hundreds—perhaps even thousands—in some countries. In Japan, if they number in the tens in one church in a year, we've experienced revival. Usually we thank God for single digits, mostly ones. The questions about why Japan and why for what sometimes seems a life sentence occasionally threaten my life as surely as someone with a knife at my heart. All the joy bleeds out and I'm left clinging precariously to a small thread of life.

By the way, God hasn't answered these questions.

Lest this sound like a pity party—not that I haven't entertained myself at many in the past—I must say that these days I'm trying to become less like Thomas and more like King David. Although he fasted and prayed one week for God to spare his son, the child died anyway. Amazingly, when David heard the sad news, he stopped weeping, got up from his prostrated position, washed, dressed, and went to the temple to worship.

David knew in the core of his being what sometimes is only in my head, despite the fact that I first gave my heart to Christ as a child. God himself explained this foundational truth in Jeremiah 29:11, "*For I know the plans I have for you, ... plans to prosper you and not to harm you, plans to give you hope and a future.*" I believe these words are true, even when everything around me contradicts them and I find myself trying to convince God that my way—not his—is best. No matter what, I want to worship God.

And what if God never answers my questions? I want to accept that too. This demonstrates ultimate trust in a loving Heavenly Father. It is also the only path to unshakable joy in this life.

Is That It!?

C. Richard Craghead

Dear God, my question is not original with me nor is this the first time we've met on this subject. The writer of Psalm 8 asks: "What is man that you are mindful of him?" The poet had already experienced your mindfulness and knew it as "caring." I was three years old when I first recognized You as a benevolent presence in my life. Cumulus clouds rolled overhead, leaving blue patches of sky through which the spring sun warmed weeds next to our house. I curled up on the weeds and imagined that You were rolling oil drums around on top of those dark clouds. For me the thunder was the noise as You cleaned up the storage shed where You had the barrels stacked. It takes a child's mind to think up that scenario.

During those early years our family had no ties with any Christian community. The closest religious influence was Dicky's mother. She was an angry atheist and would not allow us to use "cuss words" in her house. Any mention of Your name was forbidden. I don't know why she was so hostile. I felt sorry for Dicky. Thompson's epic poem *The Hound of Heaven* pictures a howling, snarling presence of You, the way Dicky's mom seemed to feel. I have been blessed from that spring day to this one with a non-stop awareness of Your presence. However, at one point I worried that I might forget Your presence.

When I was fifteen, I stayed overnight in the Catholic hospital following the removal of my tonsils. During the early morning hours I was awakened by a nun who had slipped into my room to avoid a group of penitents who were chanting as they crawled on their knees to the chapel. I asked her if she had been around when I came out from under the ether. She nodded. I had heard tales of salty blatherings that sometimes come from those who have been anesthetized. You know, O God, that I did not want to be an embarrassment to You. I asked, "Did I say anything unusual, such as swearing?" She said no. Whew! Then I burbled, "Oh, I'm so glad! You see, I just became a Christian two weeks ago and used to cuss a lot." She assured me that I had said nothing off beat and decided to leave my room.

So, you see, Divine Friend, my mind begs the question of our relationship now that I'm a "senior adult." I can look back over years of experiences with Your warm and abiding presence—both in sorrow and joy, in emptiness and fulfillment, in achievement and failure. But I'd rather not back into the future. Surely, I have not been merely a pawn played on a celestial chess board. On the other hand, surely, I have not "handled this job all by myself." Is Romans 8:28 the clearest expression of our mutuality? *In all things God works for the good of those who love him, who have been called according to his purpose.* Is that it?

Why Am I So Privileged?

Doris Aldridge Dale

While sitting in the airport in Nairobi, Kenya (East Africa), waiting to board my plane to carry me back to my comfortable home, this disturbing question arose in my mind—"God, why am I a person of privilege?" My days had been spent with some of God's choice servants in the most humble of surroundings. Pastor Moses and his wife, Beatrice, had welcomed me into their humble village, offered me hospitality and their very best, in the way of food and lodging in their beautiful country of Uganda. Their home consisted of three thatched shelters, one for the family of seven, one served as the place where meals were prepared, and one was a shelter for guests. This shelter was very modest and meager with a dirt floor, open window, and a used and rusty army cot. Luckily, I had brought along a sleeping bag which provided comfort on the rusty springs and when zipped up almost to my nose, kept the mosquitoes at bay.

After my late arrival, my hostess, Sister Beatrice, came to the door and announced that my dinner had been prepared. It was a meager handful of rice, along with some cabbage and a very small bit of chicken. There was tea, a bit of buttered bread and peanuts which are a standard at each meal. After settling for the night, I heard the beautiful sound of women's voices. A number of Ugandan sisters had followed me home and with their long abundant dresses drawn up around their chilly shoulders, sat around a fire and "stood watch" for me throughout the night. To receive their best, and to know of their love and care for me, was one of the most humbling experiences I have ever known. This has been multiplied in my journey, globally, many times.

Each time I arrive back in the US I am reminded of the "privileged" life I lead. My life is quite modest by our standards but compared to the way a major part of the world lives, it is extravagant. Sometimes, privileges cause me to be ungrateful or take for granted common ordinary gifts and conveniences. An abundance of good food, more garments than I could possibly make use of, a warm and beautiful home to share with family and friends, transportation to be accessed at will, and a community of faith that surrounds me with love and accountability. The morning I was to leave, after having been greeted by my Ugandan sisters and hosts, dear Brother Moses said to me, "The next time you visit us, dear sister, I hope to have a brick house to offer you."

One day, if I am given opportunity with my dear Lord, I hope to ask Him, "Why was I granted such privilege in this earthly life?

What Would I Ask God?

Jerry Eddy

Uh, what? God's taking questions now? And...and giving straight answers?

Why not when I was young and full of vigor? Then I could have really challenged Him. I would have come at Him with rigorous questions like Dostoyevsky's unbrotherly debate on the vexing issue of innocent suffering. Back then my middle name was Karamazov. Even the innocent suffering's more recent apologist, Rabbi Kushner, shares less than satisfying answers in *When Bad Things Happen to Good People*. Yes, I'm sure He would have had to at least clear His throat before answering that one.

And what about that "faith the size of a mustard seed" issue? Why not be more straightforward about that? I've seen too many facing the inevitability of death, which is born along with each new life, who carry either a guilty feeling that they had too little faith to bring healing or regret they didn't embrace the dying process of a spouse or a cherished loved one. How about clarifying that?

Or, not sharing the comfort of Latter Day Saints' belief, I might have asked with the poet, Eric Clapton, on the tragic death of his young son, "Will you know my name if I see you in heaven?" Ah, the real nature of the hereafter? Now, His answer to that would have been revealing.

But today I must stifle silly questions nagging to be asked, such as who really killed Kennedy and how did it happen? What really happened to those "missing" eighteen and a half minutes of the Watergate tape recording in President Nixon's secretary's office and what secrets did they contain? How in the world did Bernard Madoff scam otherwise intelligent people for almost sixty-five billion, perhaps the world's biggest ponzi scheme, and why weren't they hounding him like they would have me to collect on a fifteen dollar loan?

And yet time, experience, and engagement on a deeper level drive home the urgent need for domestic mission servants. While information and communication are exchanged at an exponentially faster pace, finding ways to address poverty of body and soul, as often as the Bible does, is still a challenge. In a greed-gripped world permeated by "what's in it for me" and the resulting casualties of an acquisitive society, my question is really rather simple. "Lord, how can I be more in this world and less of it?"

Why Doesn't God Punish Rebellion?

Deborah Zarka Miller

One of my closest friends is suffering what has become an all-American experience: the disillusion of her marriage. When someone breaks this covenant, the consequences to everyone who loves him or her are profound. Helpless to affect any positive change in this circumstance, I turn to God and demand, "Can't You do something?" And though it isn't the answer I want, God's response seems to be, "Well, what would you have Me do, Debbie?"

Of course, I don't know. Maybe I want an Old Testament God who burns cities and plagues entire nations with boils and blood water. Maybe I want God to lock this unfaithful in a house, imprisoned and starving, until he is humiliated and ready for punishment. Maybe I want God to roar in the mind of the rebellious, until she is drummed into submission, ears ringing. Maybe I want God to rip up an oak tree and wave it around in the face of every person who knows better but behaves badly anyway. Maybe I want God to stand in front of us, hands in the air, and say, "You idiot!" Or maybe I don't.

Maybe I don't want God to discipline *me* in such treacherous ways. Whenever I am tempted to rage at my children or my students or even my friends, I think about the tender, persuasive discipline one of my mentors practices so expertly with the children (and adults) in her life. When she wants to get the attention of a child who is being cruel or selfish, disrespectful or destructive, she stands very close to the child and whispers. She says that person's name, repeating it until the child hears her. Once she has the child's attention, whether reluctant or contrite, she says, "You are not a mean or ugly person. Stop what you are doing, and look at me." She never raises her voice. Sometimes, if the child flails too wildly against her authority, she simply holds onto him until he becomes still, and then she says those words again: "This is not who you are. Stop. Look at me."

I want God to discipline me, and the people I love, that way. Of course, this kind of bold compassion doesn't look like much from a distance. I think that's why God comes near when He disciplines us, so we will better understand how powerful His word, His voice, really is.

Why Was I So Afraid?

Doug Hall

God strides to the podium and invites us to take our seats. We reporters, newly arrived in heaven, shift in our chairs, competing to be noticed. God has a glint in His eye and a whisper of a smile. He's used to questions.

His gaze drifts across the pack. Suddenly, His eyes lock with mine. "You, there. Do you have a question?"

Face-to-face with the Author of All Things, I struggle to stay cool. I fumble with my notepad, mentally sorting though the questions I've composed on my journey.

I consider the first. Is this any way to run a universe? Why does God allow mental and physical illnesses that corrupt our very ability to relate to Him? Why are so many of God's children born to lives of inescapable suffering?

Or, As Creator of the universe, why don't You sign Your work? Why doesn't God write a message in the sky every morning, erasing doubts about His existence and sweeping away our tragic misunderstandings?

But, somehow, none of these questions feel like *the* question. God sees I'm having trouble.

"Step into my office," he says. "It's easier to talk there." Surprisingly, none of the other reporters object as I follow God into His den.

"What do you want to know?" He asks, sitting back and lacing His fingers behind His head. It's going to be an interview, not a simple Q&A.

I consider my indignant question about suffering. But I remember the times when I went through trouble and sensed His support, His people's support. I pause. What if I ask about the pain of others and He says, "I'm glad you cared so much. What did you do about that?" No, I'll save the question of suffering for later.

I could ask why God didn't give a clearer presentation of Himself and His message. He might respond, "Much was uncertain. Still, you knew in your heart that some things were undoubtedly right and true. What did you do with those things? Simply making something obvious doesn't change people's hearts." Maybe. Maybe not. It doesn't seem to matter so much at the moment.

The journey has been so long and I'm so tired. God knows. He spreads His arms and I collapse into the embrace of my Father. I look back on my blessings and my wounds, my generosity and my selfishness, my victories and my missed opportunities, and ask, "Why was I so afraid to act?"

What Is It That I Seek?

Don Deena Johnson

D ad had a stack of pancakes on the table in front of him and I had the house omelet that morning as we sat in a booth at Elmer's, one of Portland, Oregon's favorite breakfast restaurants. It was thirty years ago, but I still remember that place and that conversation. "How do I know God's will?" I had asked in reference to a decision regarding employment and the next steps that I should take into my future.

At that point in my life I had a rather childlike understanding of God's will, the "thou shalts" and the "thou shalt nots" of Scripture. These were, without question, God's will as put forth in His Word. And, to a certain limited extent I understood rightly. But whether through tradition, direct teaching, or the influence of family and my own distinct personality, I had come to extrapolate the right or wrong nature of God's commands to mean that all steps—all decisions were either on target or off-target. There was one right and everything else was wrong. One decision was God's will for me; all other decisions were not. One decision brought blessing, the others, punishment. Somehow, I couldn't reconcile this with what I knew about God though my question clearly indicated my desire for that one, perfectly right decision which was, in fact, the only perfect will of God. Little did I know at the time, but that question and the unrecognized nature of my agitation, would generate a lifetime of new questions, new agitation, and new pondering. What is your will, O God?

My father's suggestion that day at Elmer's, was that perhaps I could think of God's will as a broad path upon which many choices could be made. The boundaries of the path however, were clear and the path led in a particular direction toward a particular end. That thought brought huge relief to me, for it opened the possibility that there were many choices before me within God's will, not simply one. Of course, with freedom, comes responsibility and the uncertainty of many more questions without any clear answers. But that day, I was on the way toward a different sort of relationship with God—and it has made all the difference.

Sometimes, even today, I wish that there was one clearly defined and recognizable set of steps that God would describe for me in no uncertain terms. But then, of course, I wouldn't desire Him, would I? I would seek the answer, the right path, and not Him. I think God answers our question, "What is your will?" with His own question. "I am with you; are you willing to be with Me?" Thirty years ago, I wasn't ready for this answer. Today, though it isn't always what I want to hear, it suits me just fine.

What Will I Ask God When I Meet Him Face-to-Face?

Jim Lyon

It's my guess that meeting God face-to-Face will leave me speechless. The unpredictable wonder of the journey from this world to the next, the unimagined spectacle of a New Jerusalem, the magnificent Presence of my Maker (and, improbably at the same time, Savior), are enough to render any lingering question from "here below" dumb.

Still, as time (if time can there be said to still have meaning) passes by, perhaps there will be occasion to reflect, to engage in conversation with Him Who is defined by Scripture as Love, to ask for the Whys.

Suffering. Evil. Doubt. Genocide. Cancer. Mount St. Helens. The Indian Ocean Tsunami. The accident that claimed my cousin Danny's life at age nineteen. The loss of our unborn child at six months. Norman's cerebral palsy. Ted Bundy. The appalling poverty of Mumbai and Kolkata. The squalor of favellas in Rio, next door to the opulent beachfront of Ipanema. The list of imponderables is legion.

But, in the end, I don't think I would ask God to give me explanations about these. Instead, I would ask about myself. Not because I am so self-preoccupied as to be deaf to the heart cry of a struggling world, but because I intuitively know that the answer to the world's broken places is somehow woven into myself, into the mystery of fallen human nature.

Why am I, as Robert Robinson observed, *prone to wander, Lord I feel it, prone to leave the God I love?* Why would I, blanketed by faith and love, from my earliest memory, even contemplate anything else? Why would someone intellectually and deliberately surrendered into God's arms, born again, redeemed by the blood, and filled by the Spirit, still wrestle, at times, with temptation, folly, and "the flesh"? How can these things be? What's the matter with me? Why did not justification and sanctification immediately drown out the Enemy's siren and song? And, while I have often been mercifully granted victory over the devil's business, why did I even then struggle so?

The very fact that I could survive to even pose such questions past heaven's gate proves the grace of God true and supreme. Perhaps, when I arrive on "the other side," I will not wonder anymore.

O to grace how great a debtor, daily I'm constrained to be! Let Thy goodness, like a fetter, bind my wandering heart to Thee: Jesus sought me when a stranger, wandering from the fold of God; Here's my heart Lord, O take and seal it, seal it for Thy courts above.

When, by the lens of heaven, I fully comprehend myself, then, I think, I will comprehend the rest of this broken world through which we all have walked.

Who Is God Anyway?

Imy Tate Rhule

Because of my journalistic background, I find myself going to the questions of who, what, when, where, why, and how. These are all very human questions that many of us have asked over the years, but I always turn to the Scriptures when I have questions about God and my life.

Who is God? Genesis tells us that God created everything! I see God when I look out my window or see a brand new baby. The Bible also tells me that God is love. He sacrificed His life for me so that I may live abundantly and have life everlasting. 2 Corinthians 5:7 KJV says, *For we walk by faith, not by sight.* So I really don't have the question of who God is. But other questions come to mind when I think how God has worked through my life.

What is the plan for my life and where does God want me to be? At this stage in my life, I know the plan for my life. God led me to go into teaching and provided a wonderful place at Anderson University until I retired. When I have sought guidance through prayer and meditation, God has always opened avenues for me to follow.

Another human question we ask is when will the end of time come? Many have tried to prophesy this but Matthew 24:36 tells us no one knows but the Father only. The scripture also tells us to be ready.

The big questions that I have struggled with many times throughout my life are why do things happen to me and my loved ones, and how can I know God will take care of me? Why was my child severely handicapped from birth until she died? Why did my parents linger and suffer with cancer until they died? I remember when my mother was so sick, I told my dad, "When I get to heaven, I've got a lot of questions I'm going to ask God." Dad said, "You won't have any questions then." That's when I really began to understand that I didn't need to ask these questions, because no matter what happened to me, God would sustain me.

My favorite scripture that answers all questions is Romans 8:37-39 KJV. *In all these things we are more than conquerors through him who loved us. For I am persuaded that neither death, nor life, nor angels, nor principalities, nor powers, nor things present, nor things to come, nor height, nor depth, nor any other creature, shall be able to separate us from the love of God, which is in Christ Jesus our Lord.*

Universal Questions for the God of the Universe

Milan B. Dekich

*W*alk out on a clear night, look up, and you will see an amazing sight. You will see approximately two thousand stars, the edge of the Milky Way, Mars, meteors, comets, and many other spectacularly beautiful objects. Scientists estimate that the universe is at least ten billion light years across. In this universe we find nebula, a birth place for stars and black holes, collapsed stars that are so dense that not even light can escape their gravitational pull. We find quasars, comets, dark energy, dark matter, and many other mysteries.

Some questions I have for God are these: Did He create all this grandeur for our eyes only? Or are there other intelligent beings that look up into the night sky and wonder, as we do, if they are the only intelligent life God created in this vast universe? One reason I would ask God this question is this: why would He create such a glorious universe solely for us? God is a creating God. I cannot imagine that He would create such a vast and awe inspiring universe and put intelligent life on only one small planet orbiting an insignificant star in one of millions of galaxies.

We have just scratched the surface of what the universe contains. What other wonders lie beyond the horizon of what we see? Colossians 1:16 says, *For by him all things were created: things in heaven and on earth, visible and invisible, whether thrones or powers or rulers or authorities; all things were created by him and for him.* Is Paul, through the inspiration of the Holy Spirit, alluding to civilizations not only of earth but also beyond our earth? If we do discover God has put life in other parts of the universe what stories and revelations of God will they have to share with us as we share our experience of God with them? When, and if, we are able to communicate with intelligent life from other parts of this universe will we find that God will be the one experience that can unite us, just as He is the one experience that can unite the many different peoples of this earth. Maybe one day a translation of Colossians 3:11 where Paul speaks of the unity of all people in Christ will read: *Here there is no Greek or Jew, circumcised or uncircumcised, barbarian, Scythian, slave, or free **or alien life**, but Christ is all, and is in all.* (Bold italic words are the editor's addition.)

Redeeming the Past

Phyllis Gillespie Kinley

The question I recall asking in the fall when I entered fifth grade was, "God, why does this teacher hate me?" so "God, how can I make things better?" I was ten years old and I had never before been abused by an adult. I had been telling my new classmates of an experimental grade school I had attended, one associated with St. Cloud Teacher's College. I had no idea that my new teacher had attended that college and had been unhappy there.

I said nothing to my mother when the teacher pounded my fingers for mistakes in writing down answers to my math quiz. I said nothing about standing alone on the playground when classmates steered clear of me. I said nothing when she stood me before the class and called me stupid.

At first my headlong preoccupation with creating posters, book reports, and speeches for extra credit was seen only as a positive attempt to make myself at home in a new school. But after I spent weeks working feverishly until midnight to complete reports and posters, my mother confronted my teacher. Her abuse to me stopped. She had a mental breakdown that next summer. She never returned to teaching,

That question, "God, how can I make things better," because the way I dealt with life's problems as an adult. Although I learned to see how my own actions often caused problems with others, I usually returned to the question, "God how can I restore or correct this situation?"

A recent sermon by my pastor commented on Christ as "one who travels beside us to redeem the past." I was struck deeply by the promise that all those tiny, destructive sins and failures, deliberate or unknowing, those pinpricks of hurts and unfinished business are not only covered by Christ's redeeming love, but are also cancelled—forgotten and no longer in existence.

I realize that they were more than wiped out. They were, through the power of Christ's redemption, changed for good. The pastor's statement took me back to that long ago exposure to abuse.

I was filled with wonder to think that the Christ who has walked beside me almost eighty years has redeemed that past. He has not only forgiven me for any hurt I, unknowingly, caused that suffering teacher, but is also enabling me to forgive her and to forget the trauma she caused me.

Some Questions for God

Norman W. Steinaker

Thank You Lord for listening to me. I have some things I want to talk to You about. I am awed by the marvels of creation You have provided this world. Humanity is created in your image and each one of us is absolutely unique. I just don't understand it and would like to have You explain it to me.

How is it that every human being has a different DNA, a different fingerprint and footprint, and has a circulatory system which functions efficiently. Indeed, all systems of our bodies function systematically, without our even thinking about them. We grow in a prescribed fashion and develop our beings from infancy to adulthood.

I am amazed that we are provided with a brain that can think and create and do things. I personally am astonished that I can sit down and put on paper my thoughts, my hopes, my joys, my concerns, my issues, and my fears. I marvel at how my children and grandchildren learned to speak without formal training. Language is a miracle You built in to each one of us. How wonderful it is to see a child begin to articulate from initial sounds to fluent language expression. That is truly a remarkable process, but You built it into each one of us.

I have been a teacher and a writer all of my adult life. I have worked with youngsters, have watched them grow and have seen them learn from the concrete to the abstract. It is remarkable how the power of thinking linked with creative endeavor can bring something new and unique into being. I have seen it happen and it both startles and amazes me. How did You do it my Lord?

I am full of questions, but feel that You have planted within me seeds of understanding so that I will learn, when I come to be with You. About the power of Your creative genius and the creative power of Your compassion and caring. I am reminded constantly, by what I see around me, of the balance, the beauty, and the detailed nature of Your creation.

I can only marvel at what majestic creations You have in store for us when we come to be with You in that day when there is no dawning and no sunset, only the light of Your eternal presence.

"Suffer the Little Children..."

Linda Elmore Teeple

My life is woven together with countless questions. Some have found answers; some remain a mystery. A few have faded; I've made peace with the unanswerable. But there are several tenacious tendrils of wonderment wound tightly around my heart that will not untangle nor let go.

Is it a boy or a girl? I had pondered this question while pregnant with our first child. On January 26, 1977, I got my answer, but discovered that I had been asking a moot question. Our son, Jason, was delivered by emergency C-section and lived only a few hours. "God, why did my baby die? Did I do something wrong? Is my faith so flawed that I need to learn a lesson through this tragedy?"

When I went to my follow-up doctor's visit after giving birth, the only question I had for my doctor stuck in my throat like a wad of cotton. It took several attempts before he could decipher my tearful mumbling, "Did he hurt?" I suppose my question was really for God. "Did my innocent child suffer pain while in utero?"

Christmas 1977 I again was pregnant and gender was definitely irrelevant: "Is this baby healthy?" "Will my baby live—or die?" These were the questions that weighed upon my grieving yet expectant heart.

If given the opportunity to ask God one question, it would be this: "Why don't You intervene when innocent children are suffering? I understand the concept of free will in Your divine design, but can't You make an exception where children are concerned!"

As a therapist, I work with survivors of childhood traumas perpetrated (intentionally, or not) on vulnerable children. Threads of infection spider out from the wound into the far reaches of spirit and personality, disfiguring a promising future....

Notice that I did not say that the wounded person is disfigured. All of humanity is created in God's image and may be made whole by Jesus' suffering, death, and resurrection. God is in the business of reweaving the tattered shreds of our lives into something good.

When Joseph, son of Jacob, was reunited with his brothers in Egypt, he said to them, *You intended to harm me, but God intended it for good...* –Genesis 50:20.

Heavenly Father, open my heart and eyes to Your presence in the midst of suffering. May I trust that You will work it for good.

Faith Questions

Kenneth E. Crouch

*P*arents remember when their young child was full of questions. They often began with "why?" For some children the questions kept coming, especially when the answers were inadequate. As I grew older I discovered that some adults considered questions a challenge if not a threat to their authority.

Most questions went unvoiced until as a senior in high school a Sunday school teacher raised the question about the existence of the devil. Wow! Maybe there is no such being? If not, where did that idea come from? Then, from where does evil come? "So, God, is the concept of a devil necessary?"

During my first week of college I was reminded of how doubt is a necessary part of faith, a natural part of learning. But I did not have to doubt everything at once. For instance, doubt the existence of God, but hold on to a faith in Jesus.

As I questioned the existence of God, I read that monotheism is not so much that God is one, but rather God is not many. God is not an object, but spirit. Well, what is spirit? In both Hebrew and Greek, spirit is defined as breath, the energy that gives life. I have a greater respect for the mystery of God knowing how in the beginning all of the matter, energy, and potential of the universe exploded in less than a trillionth of a second from a particle smaller than an atom in a fantastic flash of light!

Questioning God is one thing but to question the church about ideas that are considered sacrosanct has often been considered heretical. Across the centuries the church has been all too willing to condemn, excommunicate, even kill the heretic. Bringing scientific evidence is not welcome if it contradicts interpretations of the Bible.

Consider how long it took the church to change its mind about slavery? Or to accept women as clergy? And how many find it difficult if not impossible to affirm the place of homosexuals in the church?

It is a joy when we find ministers, theologians, and congregations where one is allowed to question the various mysteries that intrigue. Rainer Maria Rilke wrote: "Be patient toward all that is unsolved in your heart and try to love the questions..." As a youth my pastor was Dr. Dale Oldham. On more than one occasion he said, "We do not have all of the truth, but we are committed to truth." Permission granted to seek after truth! "So, God, lead me to what is true."

Hello God!

Donna S. Thomas

*T*hanks for opening the door to heaven for me, God. This is certainly different than I ever expected. You are amazing and here I am getting to talk with You. I just don't understand it. I must be dreaming because surely it isn't me, just an ordinary human being getting to see You and even having a conversation with You. May I call You Father? I did that in all my prayers so will it still work up here? Okay?

Father, I have a lot of questions but my first one is this: You are the Creator of the world, no the whole universe. You made all the planets and stars and every thing. And then You made the world. Just look at it with all the mountains, valleys, trees, flowers, plants of every kind, thousands of different animals, and the wonderful beauty of it all. And then you made Adam and Eve and all those other people we have read about. Right now there are over six billion people all over the world. I can't even conceive how many that is.

Okay, here is my question, Father. Why, when You are so awesome and so powerful and so majestic, why do You, the Creator of the universe, care about me, one little human being? I am just one little person among all of those billions and yet You talk with me, You care for me, You have a special plan just for me, and You make special things happen for me. So Father, this is my question, Why do You care so much for me? Wow! Am I ever amazed at the attention and care You give me. This is amazing. You, the Creator of everything, care so much for me. Wow!

You said you knew me in my mother's womb too. (Psalm 139:13) You said You have Your plan for me. (Jeremiah 29:11) You said if I turn to the right or the left my ears will hear a voice behind me saying, "This is the way. (Isaiah 30:21) And now that I am a widow I can claim You as my husband. (Isaiah 54:5) I can look back over my life with total amazement at the many ways You have cared for me, led me, and had me do things I would never have dreamed.

Yes, God, uh,...Father, and what a privilege to call You Father, why do You care so much for me? Your care and love is beyond comprehension. You are wonderful. I praise You and I worship You.

Why So Much Love?

David C. Shultz

I have always believed that God loves me. In this, I was blessed more than many people are blessed. My parents were committed Christians and loving parents. My early experiences with God underscored the fact that He did, indeed love me. Saved and baptized in my eighth year, I moved through high school and college with confidence and continued to grow in my faith.

Godly professors at Warner Pacific College heightened my desire to follow God. Friends encouraged me in my quest to walk with God. My relationship with Karon Neal, now my wife of over forty years, was and still is a constant reminder of God's grace in my life.

Only many years later have I learned that my faith was based mostly on works and very little on grace. I probably responded to seventy-five percent of the altar calls given in my life. I felt I constantly needed to be better, to be more disciplined, and to be better at prayer and witnessing. I unwittingly developed the misconception that God would bless me more if I did more: more prayer, more fasting, and more commitment.

I slid into a numbing, crippling depression in the late 1980s. My endless efforts to be worthy and to work so hard God would have to bless my efforts ultimately collapsed and I found myself longing to be out of ministry. In fact, I was incapable of pastoring any more. With the gracious blessing of my congregation, I spent three months away to think and pray.

Here I finally admitted everything to myself and to God. I was tired and incapable of going on. I didn't want to be in ministry any more—ever. I wasn't sure I wanted to attend church any more. I was through! This cathartic period was immensely freeing, yet also scary. How would God respond if I rejected Him? What would I do?

Ultimately, this crisis opened the door to my most rewarding experiences with God. During the height of my emotional turmoil, God directed me to three specific verses of Scripture that He said explained how He felt about me: *I will make you like my signet ring, for I have chosen you, declares the LORD Almighty* —Haggai 2:23. *You are my son, whom I love; with you I am well pleased* —Mark 1:11. *Satan has asked to sift you as wheat. But I have prayed for you...that your faith may not fail. And when you have turned back, strengthen your brothers* —Luke 22:31.

Still I am often aghast at my ineptness and faithlessness. It seems my selfishness is unabated and my unwillingness unbounded. Yet God continues to answer my question, "Why do you love me so much?" with these words: I love you as you are. I will always love you. I am convinced He feels this way about every one of us!

Why?—Just Because!

Joy May Sherman

*W*hy me? Maybe this is the question everyone will ask God, or wants to. Why did You choose me—to love me, to set me apart, to call me into Your service? It is, after all, a very "rational" question. Not even one about "works" and "grace" either. Just a simple wondering...why me, Lord?

This is the query that creeps into my mind every Sunday before I preach, every morning when I wake up and find myself blessed with the love of a husband and child, every time I fall short of His glory and fail to meet divine expectation. It is the question that plagues me, because when I ask myself the same thing, I cannot come up with an answer.

And in this "in-between space" of earth and eternity, when my pondering becomes petition and prayer, I think I hear Him answer, but I cannot comprehend the compassion that accompanies His response. Because. Just because I love you.

Most any parent will tell you "Because!" is the answer to every "Why?" from a toddler. Especially the "whys" that have complicated counterpoints. There is comedy in the singsong questions and answers rhythm of parent-child conversation: "Why, Mommy?" "Because, Honey." "Because why, Mommy?" "Just because, Sweetheart." Back and forth it goes. And in human nature, "because" just isn't satisfactory.

So it's no wonder that when God says "because" to me, I find that answer incomplete and it makes me restless. "Because why?" I ask Him back. There has to be a reason, a rationale. It can't just "be" that way.

I think it was this same kind of legalistic, tit-for-tat, every jot and title lifestyle that confused the Pharisees and confounded the crowds when Christ interrupted their existence with a unique message from the Father: "Because He says so." All their lives these leaders and followers knew the reason for everything they did, and the consequences for not meeting expectations. Then Jesus showed up, and seemed to make His own rules.

"It is not lawful to heal on the Sabbath," they said.

"Because why?" Jesus answered. "Who told you that? Because my Father says I can...just because." "He eats with tax collectors and sinners," they said. "Why?" Jesus responds, "Because...just because I love them too."

Perhaps it is not that I seek answers to my question for God, but that I want to see His face when He answers me. Why me? Why would you let your Son die for me? Why would you love me?

"Because," He will beam. "Just because I love you." Amen.

More Awe Than Questions

Richard H. Petersen

The subject is: What question would I ask God if I had the opportunity to speak to Him? Well, I must say that I have never been comfortable with really important people. I wouldn't know what to ask the president. I cannot imagine what it would be like to be in the presence of God. I know I am always in His presence and that prayer is talking to Him, but somehow meeting Him face-to-face is beyond my comprehension.

I can relate to Job's placing his hand over his mouth (40:4). I can also relate to approaching the throne of grace with confidence (Hebrews 4:16). John's Gospel assures us that we are saved, and we shall not perish (John 3:16). But even with all this, I am not sure what I would talk about.

I will certainly remember to thank Him, for the Gospels, for the Bible, for a sound mind, and for creating me to live where I could hear the gospel and respond positively, accepting Jesus as my personal Savior and Lord. I would hesitate, looking for the right words, not wanting to sound too shallow, or lacking emotion. I think, "before Jehovah's throne," I would be more filled with awe than questions.

I have now passed my eightieth birthday. I am thankful for my family and my home church. I think about living in the South when I attended sixth grade. Did that make me, born a Connecticut Yankee, more sensitive to feelings of those who experienced segregation? I think of my older sister's death. She was nineteen. I was four years younger than she. Did that keep me, a teenager, thinking about God?

When I was a young man, I was a sales engineer. Did this experience help me gain self-confidence? God led me through a perilous period in human history. What was He doing that led me safely to my wonderful wife and marriage of now fifty-eight years? How did He reach me with His gospel? Was it a radio program with Billy Graham peaching on *The Hour of Decision,* or the constant reminder, week after week, of the Scriptures being read in the church services? I'll join the choir.

Praise God, from whom all blessings flow; Praise Him, all creatures here below; Praise Him above, ye heavenly host; Praise Father, Son, and Holy Ghost. Amen.

When Will the Answer Come?

Helen Jones Newell

"You have a son." "He has his mother's eyes." "Will he become a pastor like his father?"

That joy soon turned to anxiety. The breach delivery with weight over ten pounds was difficult resulting in severe brain hemorrhage. He may develop hydrocephalus. We had never heard of such birth problems in 1953. Wild stories invaded us.

Family, friends, and the church prayed. We believed that God honors His saints, answering their prayers. Time passed. Answers did not come. "God, why not?" Headaches developed. Faith turned to doubt. "Is it my fault?" "What did I do wrong?" Is there hidden sin? Soul searching revealed nothing. I had always obeyed what the church taught. Doubt turned to suspicion. Had Arlo committed unconfessed sin during the war?

Weeks, months went by. There were repeated hospitalizations but no progress until the doctor determined to do a lumbar shunt that would relieve the fluid. Arlo was in Essen, Germany, for the World Convention in 1959. When our youth pastor chose not to go to Lake Lure Youth Camp, I felt responsible. The children and I drove to camp in the mountains, two hundred miles from High Point. Two days later we went to the hospital in Winston-Salem. Arlo returned, arriving at the hospital the afternoon of the surgery.

Was this God's answer? Now there was a ray of hope. "God, were You trying to teach me something? What?"

Early in 1960 the church in St. Louis called us. This farm girl had never lived in the city. "God, how do I know if You are really calling us?" Will there be adequate medical facilities, a more important concern than a new parsonage or what the church expected of me? March 27 was our first Sunday. What a gracious, loving congregation.

The surgeon in North Carolina contacted one in St. Louis making the transition easier. The doctor suggested a new procedure, a Holter Valve placed in the neck. Two months later kidney failure resulted in one being removed. This was the last of the surgeries.

Little did we know the anguish Rick would endure when others made fun of his speech and his walk. It grew worse in high school and college. That was not the end. Believing that God had called him into a pastoral ministry, he faced repeated discouragement. Churches would not have a pastor with a speech impediment.

Parents can be biased, but real joy comes now when a parishioner tells us, "Your son has the heart of a true pastor."

A Few Big Questions

Gene W. Newberry

*D*ear Heavenly Father,

Thank you for welcoming us home. I had a couple of teasing little questions that have bugged me all my mortal life. One, how did old Methuselah make it to 969, when most of us, if we make it to 90, use a walker or cane for our taxing arthritis or take a fistful of pills for our cardiac problem? Two, why didn't Noah clobber the two malarial mosquitoes as they tried to enter the ark? These may be trivial questions, but I'm serious in asking them.

Now God, here is the poser, my biggest question: Explain the spiritual dimension of life to me. On earth, we were caught up in the physical, the material, and barely experienced the spiritual. It was mysterious, mystical, transcendental.

We prayed and meditated but weren't sure we were getting through. Now the physical is gone, and we have a body fit for the new world of the spirit. Now we stand before You, also spirit, in awe and reverence, in what seems our eternal destiny. Time, space, and physicality appear unnecessary and are gone. We know we will be looking up to You for wisdom and counsel.

Close to the big question are these nettlesome ones. What about the relationships we know on earth, like marriage, family, friendships, and the vocations we pursue? Do we sit at tables for food and drink? Where are the wonders of conversion and the church, worship, and music we loved so much? What about the objects and activities that made life pleasant and fulfilling? I'll name a few: books, automobiles, houses and buildings, clothing, universities, travel, and more.

Dear God, we know we'll stand in awe of Your glory, love, and power. However, we can't help asking what we change and what we gain in the new spiritual and paradisiacal world with You. What are heaven and eternity like? The dearest things on earth are family, friends, and church. We can't help but ask if the heavenly venue and program will contain these.

But the greatest mystery and quest of all is to bow before the heavenly Father in humility and awe and drink in the meanings of spirit, love, and eternal life.

It Really Is That Simple

Juanita Evans Leonard

When I retired two and a half years ago, ready to explore a new life, in a new community, little did I know what God had in mind. What a sense of humor—me in water aerobics. New friends, through YMCA classes, have been sent by God as a lifeline to new horizons.

Women and men over seventy and several well into their eighties and nineties have become wells of wisdom for me.

These water nymphs have been so important to my becoming "southernized." It has been quite a fun and comfortable process as my new teachers have answered so many questions about the city, politics of the community, where to attend church, and what doctors and dentists to see.

Yes, there have been questions of me—are you a teacher—a pastor? Are you married? Do you have children? Would you answer a theological question for me? Would you go to lunch? There are a few professional questions I would like to have your reaction to.

It seems we humans are full of questions about a myriad of issues. They come throughout the life span no matter where we live on the planet. We ask them of each other and we ask our Creator.

For example, Miss Billie is in her late eighties. She and I share a water aerobics class at the local YMCA. Recently we met after class at the front desk. She asked me if I would pray for her during eye surgery to remove a cataract. "Sure, but I want to ask *you* a question. Miss Billie, I have a writing assignment about questions to ask God. What would you say?" "Well there are the usual questions like—Why did my child have to die? Why did my companion die so young? What will I do when the unemployment runs out? My friend, you know the rest of the questions. However, now we see through the glass darkly but then we will see (know) face-to-face. Nita, it will not matter."

"Thanks Miss Billie."

It really is that simple.

A Cloudy Picture in a Mirror

James H. Bailey

It was a dream. My questions were answered, yet they weren't. Nothing is resolved in a dream.

As I emerged from a tunnel, the light was so great I couldn't look at it. A gentle voice beckoned me forward.

"Welcome home, Jim," the voice said. "Is this heaven?" I asked. "Yes," the voice replied. "There is much you cannot be expected to understand. But I will explain." "Lord, You are too great to comprehend," I said softly. "How can I communicate meaningfully with You?" The voice answered, "From the beginning a way was planned for the communion of Creator and creation." The light softened, and out stepped a man. "Jesus Christ!" I said. And I wasn't cussing.

"Glad to see you, Jim," he said. "Now, what are you wondering about?" I collected my thoughts. "I admit that on the occasions I faced my own mortality, I had strange doubts. Was this all there is? Is there really a hereafter? No one ever came back to confirm a heaven, so I never could be sure." "Humans never are sure of things they cannot see," Jesus explained. "Blessed are they who have believed without seeing."

I continued. "I believed in You as the son of God. And in the Holy Spirit. But that is hard to comprehend. Are You and God the same?"

He smiled. "How do you see God?" "As the author of all that is good, even encompassing it."

"Just so," he replied. "Picture God as a person and people as ants. How would you reach the ant world? Thus I became a person. And after I left, relationships became spiritual." I had other concerns. "I've survived a crisis or two. But I was left fatherless at eleven. You healed his cancer, but he died anyway. Then my closest cousin was asphyxiated in a camping accident at twenty-six. Why?" Jesus smiled. "It's hard to see the big picture when things happen to those close to you. As we go on, I'll explain."

"First I'd like to see my family," I said. "Fine, how about now?"

"Will I know them?" I asked. "Of course. And they'll know you, even though they haven't seen you recently. Here we are not known by the physical attributes of our earthly bodies."

I'm sure I'll come to understand it when I get there. As the Apostle Paul said, *Now all we can see of God is like a cloudy picture in a mirror. Later we will see him face to face* —1 Corinthians 13:12 CEV.

By then I'm sure I'll have even more questions. And He will have the answers.

Why Such Love?

Laura Withrow Hoak

The questions I wrestle with today in this complicated, often unfair world may seem as nothing when I reach that home beyond this life. Passing to the other shore may be a little like crawling into a warm, comfortable bed at night after a long and grueling day, when one simply sinks with gratitude into the soft folds of the blankets and breathes a gentle sigh of relief. The joy of finally reaching what we choose to call heaven may be so overwhelming that questions will seem superfluous.

Some things that bother me today—why do innocent children have to suffer, why does death have to be a part of life, why do we so easily succumb to evil when good is so very near at hand, why does life often seem unfair—are unanswerable in this life and with my limited knowledge. The books I read and especially God's Word, the Bible, give some insight, but mostly the questions return in the continuing saga of life. I am thinking that in eternity we will naturally understand, or maybe it will not matter then.

Maybe though, after a moment of rest, I still will have one question: Why does God always have such magnanimous love for us when we so often behave like spoiled children? We, as humans, seem to be caught in a web of self destruction from which we are unable to free ourselves. We fight among ourselves, judge others as wrong simply because they are different from us, grab material possessions as if they were the stuff of life, mistreat our own bodies for self-gratification—inventing ways to reject the generous, unending love of the Father.

When I consider the wondrous world God has made, I am reminded that He has already placed at our fingertips the resources to answer many of our questions. Food enough and to spare is available when feeding our neighbor is as important to us as feeding ourselves. Energy resources are in abundant supply if we recognize that our fair share may be less than we have imagined. The beauty and order of our world is food enough for our spirits to last a lifetime.

In spite of our bungling, wayward ways, God's love continues, calling us back, over and over again, to Himself, the constantly loving, ever forgiving Parent. Why He loves us so much is a question I may want to ask someday, except that when I am at home with God for eternity, it may be unnecessary.

God Almighty Questions

Sam Collins

I could ask any of a number of questions that have been asked of God down through the ages: Why is there evil? Why do good people suffer? How many angels can dance on the head of a pin—and is there enough room for a full orchestra, or do the cherubs have to hum their own accompaniment?

Some folks believe that God is going to clear up all of our wondering in the great hereafter. Like a divine version of a presidential news conference, God's press secretary is going to step into a celestial briefing room and announce, "The Almighty will now take your questions."

I think that expectation is off the mark. For one thing, if the Bible is any indication, God often seems more inclined to ask questions than to reply to them in definitive detail.

After having his life and fortune shredded like an old sweater tossed into the middle of a dog fight, Job raised so many questions that it would have taken a committee of theologians and Oxford-educated philosophers a couple of decades just to catalog them. When God finally deigned to show up, the Creator did not go point-by-point and set Job's mind at ease or provide the page number of the answer key printed in the back of the Good Book. Instead God announced, *Brace yourself like a man; I will question you, and you shall answer me* —Job 38:3—then God reeled off his own staggering list of questions.

God's response to Job is consistent with the picture of God presented in much of the Bible and even in the person of Jesus Christ. Throughout the New Testament, Jesus often sounded like a *Jeopardy* contestant, constantly framing his responses—to adversaries, to disciples, to members of his own family—in the form of questions.

Could it be that God's questions are far better and more applicable to real life than the supposedly divinely-inspired answers pushed by many cocksure fundamentalists, liberal theologians, and self-designated wise heads? Rather than God's answers, it is often God's questions that humble us; nudge us down the road less traveled; provide us with perspective; cause us to stop short, puzzle, ponder, and change direction.

I am increasingly convinced that God is less interested in having me embrace the answers provided by religious "authorities" and more keen on having me ferret out and live in the framework of His questions. So my question is simply this: In the midst of my searching, bafflement, and angst, Almighty God, what questions do you have for me?

Wonderings

Christa Sterken

*M*any question God. Longing for answers about suffering, sin, and tragedy. In the midst of that I wonder...
How could I miss You in the ordinariness of life, God?

I am stunned by the artistry of God. It has become second nature to keep looking for it, stopping to live purposefully and appreciate it. Second nature is not enough for me.

I would ask how His creation, His masterpiece in human existence, could be marred by lack of observation about His other works?

People are often surprised when I ask what they love most about the day. Too often I miss it myself.

There are times when the search must become more exhaustive, when the beauty is elusive. Recently our daughter spent time in the hospital in extreme pain. The experience was the worst of my life. Yet, as I lay awake in her room at night, the discipline of looking for the details paid off.

I was tired and full of heartache for her suffering. Her cries were something no parent should ever hear. Yet I trusted God. I looked around the room, desperate for a ray of hope. Suddenly, the hospital overhead speakers announced a prayer for all hospital staff; praying for God to guide their hands, protect their patients, and for the glory to be given to Him. I sat motionless for a moment.

Peace swept over me and I was reminded of God's promises to prosper not to harm. I looked around the room and realized how comfortable we were made to feel in this entirely uncomfortable situation. How the doctors were able to find medicine to alleviate her pain enough for her to rest that night, how much we had to be thankful for in the midst of a difficult circumstance. Robust hymns were piped in every four hours to remind nurses to care for their patients. Once I started searching, the unlikely beauty of our surroundings became apparent.

Once home again, the standard duties of life threatened to sabotage my appreciation of details I had worked so hard to notice. Being grateful for things doesn't seem to be an attribute that always comes naturally. But I will keep trying, it is worth it.

God forgive me when I miss it, forgive us all. You are good, all the time...whether we recognize it not. Thank you.

"O God, Why?"

Frederick D. Clemens

After completing college and seminary, I began my ministry. I married Linda and helped her finish nurse's training—all according to plan! Next, we planned our family. On May 29, 1980, our son, Adam Frederick, was born—all according to plan. But plans were derailed when Adam died at birth—my plans had *not* included stillbirth. Twenty-two days later Linda died. I was extremely angry! The most important people in my world were gone.

I knew anger was a normal reaction. Kubler-Ross writes: "Feelings of anger, rage, envy, and resentment [are common at death]. The logical next question becomes 'Why me?'...this stage of anger is very difficult to cope with from the point of view of the family and staff." [*On Death and Dying*, 1969, p. 50] With that awareness, I focused anger at God. "O God, why? Why me? Why now? Adam did not deserve this. Linda did not deserve this...nor did I.

I used my anger for energy to write the article: "Stillbirth: A Father Speaks." But questions remained: Why? Confusion caused me to wonder if God was withholding God's blessings from us for reasons not clear to me. But to my mind, there was *no* good reason why this happened.

I knew some babies are stillborn. But surely this was not the reality being forced on me. Adam had done nothing to deserve such a tragic beginning and ending to his life.

Time passed.

Three years later I married Becky. Within five years, we lived with three pregnancies and miscarried each time. "O God, not this time!"

Questions have been many. Answers have come like molasses—so very slowly...if at all. But understanding has surfaced in ways not satisfying others, but these answers are helping to dissipate my disappointment and quiet my mind.

For one thing, these things happen. Current research notes one in four pregnancies end in miscarriage. Other research records a one in three rate of miscarriage. By these numbers, a couple is more likely to face a miscarriage than a ballplayer is to bat .300.

Still, other questions come to mind. As Christian believers many affirm the fact of faith which assures us. "With God all things are possible." Has there been a problem with our faith? I still wonder!

Simplifying God

Kathryn Womack-States

ometimes I complicate the easy. When asked to ponder a "sit down" with God, my complicated self emerged and so did my need for pre-conditions. Enter my mind here at your own risk. Wouldn't I need an image of God? I thought. Would God look like George Burns? Morgan Freeman? Della Reese? Opie Taylor? Wait!! I can't print that...If there was anyone left who didn't know I'm a dork that would settle it...Why did I agree to do this? I don't know what God looks like, and even if I did, we'd have to have a place to...Hey, where would I meet God? Would it be a church, or a front porch...maybe a mountain or the beach? Perhaps we'd meet at Starbucks....

It was about here that I realized that I hadn't even gotten to the assignment: settling on "a question." The profound inquiries have all been asked by those smarter than me, I mused. Then, things got more complicated. Every question I posed required a picture or setting change. I can't ask George Burns that question in church!! Finally, I blurted out: "God, why do I have to make things so complicated?" In my pause, the sacred response came graciously and playfully when I heard—"I don't know."

So, here is my do over. Plain truth: I find it difficult to imagine a back and forth conversation with God. My image of the Divine is no longer the white-bearded old man on a throne in the heavens. My view of God is indefinable and frankly indescribable. Don't get me wrong, I see God everywhere. I see God in the breath-taking beauty of nature. I see God in the faces of others who love and accept me beyond my understanding. I experience God as a sacred, encompassing presence. Come to think of it, I often ask questions of God. In times of uncertainty, when I yearn for direction, my soul asks for guidance. One thing I know for sure—No matter the setting or form...God is always present in each moment, and now that I think about it, what is so complicated about that?

So Many Questions, So Few Years

Arthur R. Eikamp

Why did You make a world with tectonic plates that push against each other and when they slip there is an earthquake? Why did You make a world at all? Why did You put me in this world? Why did You put anyone in the world? When there is an earthquake, what do You really want me to do?

Since You had no mother or father Yourself, where did You get the wonderful idea of parents and children and families? You knew that family members would sometimes disagree and even quarrel but still be bound together for life. Did You maybe give us the family as a pattern for the family of God—the church?

Are my mom and dad really with You there? If they are, would You please tell my mom how sorry I am that I didn't tell her what a great mom she was while she was still here with us? If there really is a heaven, what do people do there all the time? My pastor seems to indicate that only Christians go to heaven. That leaves me with a question only You can answer. What happens to all the Hindus, Muslims, Buddhists, and others whom You also created? If maybe, some of them at least, go to heaven along with the Christians, do they get along any better there than they do here?

Where do animals fit into Your scheme of things? Are there any special arrangements for cats and dogs that have often been so faithful to us here? Did You create dogs in order to show people what loyalty is?

How about history? Does it move in any particular direction? Does it just repeat itself over and over? Does anyone outside of You know?

Do You remain a mystery to us humans to make us stretch to even try and touch the hem of Your garment? Is it to let us know that no matter how much we stand on tiptoe and stretch, our arms will always be too short?

Finally one little silly question: How do I fix my computer?

Thank You for giving me ninety wonderful years of life here on earth. Is there anything special You want me to do with whatever few years I may have left?

Why Do You Love Us?

Risë Wood Singer

The Father has loved us so much that we are called children of God. And, we really are His children. —1 John 3:1 NCV

Mankind? Have you ever taken a good look at us? Are we pretty? No! Do we behave well? Not most of the time. Are we nice? Sometimes. Are we loveable? Seldom.

I hate to go to the grocery store. It's humankind at its worst. Something weird always happens at the grocery store. Either old men ask me where to find olives or there is a Spanish-speaking woman screaming at her seven uncontrollable kids while they throw eggs at each other. Or, I have to listen to a couple fighting or see underwear hanging out of falling-off, baggy britches. And, then after my lovely shopping experience, I get in the "quick" check-out line behind a very large odiferous, toothless woman with *way* more than ten items, wearing no undergarments, trying to figure out her food stamps. These times are not on my list of "fun things to do."

When I *finally* get to pay for my ten items and am back to my car, I have to calm myself before I actually feel safe to operate this potentially lethal piece of machinery. *Then* is when I find myself asking, "How could all these people be called children of God and *why* does He love us?" And, trying *not* to judge by appearance only, I still look around as I go about my life, and I have to face the fact that humankind is ugly, inside and out; downright unattractive, rude, mean-spirited, abusive, filthy in word and deed, and in out-of-shape, pierced, tattooed bodies with not enough clothes on them. And yet, we still are God's children and He loves us.

What I see is visually relatively accurate, *but* it's not how God sees us! Even if we all *looked* good, many still fail miserably as they stumble around directionless with no intention of finding their way. Sadness and grief is overwhelming and hate and sickness thrive and grow into war and death. We bumble through this life making huge mistakes and deplorable choices causing Him much grief and disappointment. *Why* does He continue to love us and call us His children?

Even as I ponder the wonder of His love, I know that if the *only* person that *ever* lived was the woman in front of me at the grocery store, Jesus would have died for just her. Is our love for our children conditional, based on what they do and say? Sadly, sometimes it is. Thankfully, that's not true with God, our Father. I *know* He continues to love us, I just don't know why.

How Are We Doing?

Raymond A. Freer

You gave artists the gift of being able to create—bringing ideas and inspiration to the life of the church in Your world. Painters gave life to Bible stories on woven canvasses, intricately crafted with brushstrokes and vibrant colors. Beautiful glass enhanced by sunlight filtering through stained windows has facilitated worship experiences. Luminous marble has been carved lovingly by sculptors. Clay has been formed with the upmost care by potters. Artists were given and have used this gift in amazing ways, but I wonder if we have used our creativity wisely?

In the first millennium and a half since the Christ event, artisans relied heavily on Biblical themes for their subject matter. Most successful artists were commissioned by the church to create works that helped the viewer visualize the scriptures. How did they do when interpreting Your message of joy and hope? Was honor and glory given to Your name? Are You pleased with attempts to tell Your story? Or was sacred art misused to control the thinking and actions of the parishioners? Did the point of view of patrons ever cloud the message or mislead the viewer?

Franz Marc (1880-1916) stated that "Thoughts and feelings about a Supreme Being still provide food for the arts." I wonder if spiritual energy is still the primary force in art? Has the influence of sacred art lost its power to enrich our lives and provide sustenance because of its familiarity? Or would the absence of sacred art make a difference in the worship experience of seekers?

Cathedrals, mosques, and churches are timeless, spectacular architectural achievements, inspiring worshipers throughout the ages. Those of us who feel compelled to respond to Your message believe that visual representation and imagination is pleasing to You. However, was our quest to capture and elaborate upon Your inspiration pleasing in Your sight or were we instead erecting monuments to our own creativity and losing our focus on You, the Creator?

Meaning in the Journey

Carma Withrow Wood

He was my mentor, my first example of a man, my father, my daddy. As a teenager he left an abusive home for the inviting warmth of a church family ready to embrace and affirm him. By leaving his birth family he severed ties that would become a thread of bittersweet growth, pain, and redemption woven throughout his lifetime. He set his face toward a calling that would sustain him through all of the transitions, challenges, and joys of living.

He had a wonderful mind, insatiable in its need to continue learning, with a desire to reach an understanding on a broad range of subjects: theology, history, psychology, sociology, geography, and current events.

In circles of leadership he had the reputation of being something of a hardhead. Some called him stubborn or argumentative. But, his work ethic and integrity earned him great respect even from his critics. He was able to articulate and synthesize information with the most educated among us. Yet, he had a great disdain for pretense and what he called "saccharin" in any form when it came to communication and the living out of faith. He was direct and uncompromising in the mantle of leadership he felt in his many roles of service and vocation. And, among his peers, he intentionally sought out the inexperienced and least influential to lend a listening ear and a voice of encouragement.

Yet, in the final eight years of his life, this dynamic servant leader was stricken with a debilitating disease that cut short what had promised to be a fruitful retirement. There had been hopes of short terms of service to the church; leisurely adventures with the love of his life to places yet unseen; and writing, yes, always more writing. All of these remain undone...grandchildren's graduations and weddings unattended...great-grandchildren who will not know their great-grandfather's silly sense of humor...dreams and hopes cut short by an illness that took his body and ruthlessly chipped away at his spirit.

Have You prepared a place for my dad? Will there be a healing between the father, mother, and son, a relationship that had so long ago been broken? Is there time and opportunity for him to banter with the apostle Paul? Are his legs once again strong and youthful walking on golden streets with a spring in his step?

Lord, I thank You for the mercy of taking him home and pray for a day when I will see through Your eyes the meaning of this journey.

What Is Fair?

Barry F. Hoffman

*W*hy do some babies have to struggle to live and others are perfectly healthy?

Why are some babies born to unhealthy families? Why are some parents unable to have children, even though they want them and would provide good parenting?

As a grandparent, I had some of these questions on my mind as I looked upon my grandson five years ago. He was a tiny human being fighting for his life with every breath he took. During the first five months, spent in the hospital's Pediatric Critical Care Unit, he faced many challenges in his young life. Five life-threatening operations were a part of his life before he left the hospital.

Standing there vigilant at the side of his bed were his parents who were responsible for saving his life—one of the two times his heart stopped by immediately notifying the hospital personnel. Their loving strength, gentle touch, and firm advocacy on my grandson's behalf helped support him in surmounting the recovery process. They were there for him—using their blend of music, touch, smiles, talk, and hugs.

As I looked around me, I saw many other parents doing the same for their babies who were struggling for survival. Although I never received an answer to the question about why some babies have to struggle to survive, I saw God working to bring health and wholeness to these babies in a number of ways. God's help was there through the many prayers of a community of Christian love. God helped through the love and support of the parents, grandparents, family, and friends as they surrounded Dylan and the other babies who were grasping life and breath. God was present through the skills of the physicians and the constant loving care of the nurses.

Dylan today is a lively, energetic, and sensitive person who brings love and joy to his family.

In addition, he has the possibility of future operations, but God in Christ is there through the power and presence of the Holy Spirit who brings comfort and strength to everyday challenges and provides us with the resources to cope with the questions of life.

What Would I Ask God?

Margaret Jones Smith

The four-year-old child asks, "Why is the sky blue? Why is the grass green?" or in other words, "What is my future? How should I prepare for the Now? These questions are asked over and over through the years, only they are expressed in the words relating to the challenges of our life changes. The questions through the years relate to career, then marriage and family, then the welfare of the grown children, and then the postretirement career.

My sixteen-year-old question was the choice of college and career preparation. God answered that prayer and added the question of whom I should marry at the same time. God continued to answer my questions as I tried to prepare the children for their futures. The three score years passed so quickly, and then the question for purposeful living in the career during retirement was an urgent plea. God heard all these questions through the years. God's patience and caring never ceased to amaze me.

Then there was widowhood. I had not asked for that terrible loneliness. God heard my anguish in the question, "What is there for me to live for? God give me a purpose for living." Again, God was patient, and one day at a time, led me toward a future.

The years have now become fourscore plus. Each day is a gift. I do not make long-range plans, but I do want to live a purposeful life each day. So every morning in my meditations, my question is, "God, what do you have waiting for me today?" God answers with wonderful surprises. Yes, I continue to ask, "Why is the sky blue? Why is the grass green?"

Grading Our Tragedy

James L. Sparks

Like most folks, I've known some dark times: a prodigal daughter who spent years in the "far country," a wife of a staff member who betrayed her marriage vows, a mother-in-law who spent years in the fog of dementia, colleagues who judged me, friends who surprised me, congregations who ridiculed me, and a doctor's diagnosis that scared me.

After sharing some thoughts on tragedies, a congregational member approached me with her belief: "You don't know a thing about tragedy! Your experiences were nothing! Let me tell you about heartache!" And she began to list her tale of woe. To be honest, if half of what she said was true, her life experience has been bleak. I expressed sympathy to her and commiserated over her misfortune.

But to be fair, all tragedy is tragic. My mother-in-law, who experienced the issues of dementia for over five years, knew tragedy, but my wife, who was her primary caregiver, watched her mother exiting by inches. Which is worse? My father lingered in a coma for weeks before death; my mother stopped reading a book, bowed her head and died. Which mode of death is more severe? For the past three years I've been walking with a friend who is battling cancer, feeling little hope for a long-term release, while another friend was killed by a drunk driver. Which experience is more difficult to bear? In the quiet morning light I bow in prayer, asking for God's help to face the dangers of the day, and in the darkness of night I grimace in reflecting upon the difficulties I faced in the day. And I realize that all tragedies are tragic; there is no variance or spectrum or grading scale.

I've come to believe that all of us—in pain or anger or frustration or weariness—have shaken our fists at the heavens and cried out "Why?" In Matthew 5:45 RSV, Jesus teaches us that God *sends rain on the just and on the unjust*. The experiences of our lives bear that out. Yet as common as the calamities of our lives is the abundance of God's grace. There is a certain peace that comes with understanding and accepting God's sovereignty. There is in every life both joy and pain, blessing and tragedy, elation and sorrow. And I feel there should be. The *rain* that falls is, more often than not, a pouring out of grace during days of difficulty.

I've learned to stop "grading" my pain. It all hurts, and it hurts us all!

Dear God, Who Are You, Really?

Kay Murphy Shively

"God is Love" was one of the first things I was taught as a child. I'm sure I could repeat it before I ever had any idea what it meant. In fact, more than sixty years later, I'm still not altogether sure.

The problem is, God, that who You are—or were said to be—got complicated. For I also learned this little song: *O be careful little hands what you do, for the Father up above is looking down in love...* Those words didn't make me feel loved. They made me feel...watched. And it wasn't a comfortable feeling.

And then I learned that You could be angry—even violent. People's wickedness made You so angry that You destroyed everyone except Noah and his family. (And that brings up another question: Did You ever really look at Noah? That man was no saint! Why was he saved, while innocent babies who had never even had the chance to sin, died?)

All through the Bible, I find conflicting pictures of You. One writer says, "The steadfast love of the Lord never ceases; his mercies never come to an end." Another says, "God so loved the world..." On the other hand, You told the Israelites to move into an occupied land and wipe out the original inhabitants. If You love the whole world, why was that fair? And You even "destroyed without mercy all the dwellings of Jacob." Even Your own chosen people weren't safe from Your wrath.

Some people argue that in my finite (and sinful) foolishness, I can't possibly understand You, so I shouldn't question. They suggest that, since You are God, You can be all of these things at once. You are entitled to the wrath and vengeance. But to me, that doesn't seem like love. And so, like Job, I will contend with You.

Are You the God of Hosea, the One of infinite compassion, or the God of consuming wrath pictured by Nahum? Are You the God of peace, as Micah proclaims, or the vengeful warrior of Obadiah?

Then there's Jesus. If the Son is the reflection of the Father, are You as loving as Jesus? Is it possible that, for centuries, You have been misunderstood and misrepresented as wrathful and vengeful? Jesus said that to know Him was to know You. He chose mercy over vengeance, compassion over judgment, peace over war. May I dare to believe that this is who You are, really?

On Our Own?

J. Paul Vincent

The existentialists say that no person can live your life or die your death for you, but everyone knows that no person can grow old for you either. So, I'm having to do it on my own.

Meryl Streep once said that in the late-life romance of a good marriage you "love without looking." At least the times when "looking" seemed everything have receded into more placid days when the amorous tumults of youth come more mildly and fitfully.

The move from middle-aged vitality to "golden senior" status seems to make for little good except the discount coupons to Big Boy. Women my age observe their skin change from silk to flannel and blue veins surface to worm their way under age spots and over arthritic bones and knuckles. Such creatures hope the makeup has done the trick, but no tricks can restore the glory. Male peers are little better off, learning quickly that slack muscle tone and wrinkles are not gender-specific. Graying and thinning hair is desperately swept up and over the bald spot like a breaking wave on a desolate beach.

Recently our local television station carried a lead story about an "elderly" woman and her selfless involvement in a volunteer service project. Waiting through the commercial break for more details, I found that the woman was *sixty*. In the dizzy blitz of the youth culture, we retirees stumble about like aliens from some forgotten subcontinent of nostalgia. The AM playlist, even the "top ten," is a catalogue of strange names and unfamiliar songs. What is thought funny has undergone a mutation; our children don't "love" Lucy, and they manage only polite, puzzled smiles at Red Skelton or Jack Benny. And, of course, that breakfast restaurant with the endless refills of coffee and toasters at each table is closed; fast-food franchises line the strip providing food in disposable paper containers.

God knows why the knees ache and the head throbs, why the room turns like a child's pinwheel when we rise too fast. A day will come when He will answer even our tiresome questions about bunions and shingles. Until then, God does not withhold Himself from us, and we are never really on our own.

Gatsby dreamed of holding back the summer and repeating the past, but God's will is something better: Every moment His will can be done on earth as it is in heaven.

"Cut"

Jeanette Morehead MacMillan

How can a person who is at peace with You suffer from an anxiety disorder? God, I'd like to share the story with You, which prompted my question.

I was the media specialist at a middle school when asked: "Mrs. MacMillan, does our school library have the book, *Cut*?"

"No, Ruth, but I'll consider ordering it." Aware of what the subject matter was, I drew in a breath as I quickly glanced at her arms. The jagged, reddish scabs, which looked like a cat had clawed her, confirmed my suspicion. This was her cry for help.

Prior to ordering the requested book I read this review: "The story of Callie who cuts herself. Never too deep, but enough to feel the pain, enough to feel the scream inside." After reading the book and discussing it with the guidance counselor, we decided it would be helpful to Ruth. When she checked it out, I casually asked if she wanted to share her interest in the book. Tearfully she shook the long, black strands of hair out of her eyes and explained that she used the same escape method to ease her anxiety, but no one seemed to understand. She was bright and attractive, so we'd been unaware of her misery.

When Ruth returned from rehab, I saw her often, as she was an avid reader. Her arms healed and her smile returned; however she confided: "It's hard and I have a long way to go."

The school year ended and she graduated from eighth grade. I often wonder if Ruth has been able to control her anxiety, or if it's controlling her.

I'm not sure what Ruth's relationship with You was. However, at about the same time, a young woman in our church was having extreme anxiety attacks. I became aware of it when I noticed the terrible scratches on her arms. She'd dedicated her life to You. She loved children and was a gifted teacher. She was outgoing and was loved and trusted by everyone. However when alone, she couldn't control her anxiety. In Philippians 4:6 and 7 NLT, Paul wrote: *Don't worry about anything, instead pray about everything. Tell God what you need, and thank Him for all He has done. Then you will experience God's peace, which exceeds anything we can understand. His peace will guard your hearts and minds as you live in Christ Jesus.*

God, if Paul was correct, why does anxiety control some of Your faithful children?

Salvation to Other Cultures?

Jim B. Luttrell

*L*ife is a drama. In this drama God is the audience, the Holy Spirit is the director, and we are the characters in the cast.

What God desires from us is worship and service, and when we are in service we can forget about our doubts because we are caught up in giving—giving God our praise and giving to others at their point of need. That brings an inner peace and satisfaction that defies doubt.

Questioning is not necessarily a doubt but demonstrates a lack of understanding and a need for enlightenment. The truth is that we all suffer from the "Adam and Eve" syndrome. In other words, we want to know the mind of God. Since we are mere humans how else can we learn the discipline and principles of trust which are basic to Christian faith?

God, Your Word says that "all persons are created equal," and also that no one comes to the Father except by Me" (Jesus Christ). The resulting question based upon these biblical statements becomes a spiritual enigma. Since no one can access You except through Jesus Christ, how do You relate to, reveal Yourself, and communicate with those in other cultures and faiths in such a way as to allow them the choice of eternal salvation?

The rationale relating to this question is that certainly God would not create an entire culture or group of human beings, only to have them miss out on eternal salvation. Would God do that? Certainly a God who loves us all equally and cares for all people could not be true to His nature by creating persons who have no possibility of salvation or of establishing a personal relationship with God Almighty!! So, "How do You do that, God?"

Wisdom is the proper application of knowledge and experience. My wisdom tells me that God, indeed, cares for all peoples and that He has His own way of communicating with all.

The question in my survey responses which showed the most wisdom to me was this: "What one thing can I do for You which would please You the most?" This is a totally unselfish question and focuses upon God, not ourselves.

The bottom line for believers is the realization that God does, indeed, exist, and God is fully and ultimately good, and He is the maker, preserver, and the hope of the universe and all of its inhabitants.

Enlightenment

Lolly Bargerstock-Oyler

When I was in college, I kept a mental list of my top ten questions for God. Eventually, I dropped the list as it grew mentally burdensome to carry around. For me, writing about my questions for God is a bit like writing about the times I have slept, or eaten, or taken breath. Questions are ever present and rarely have I been able to rest in an "answer." In some sense, resting in the unknown has become a way of life.

Having been asked to write on the topic of questions for God, I obsessed to find the one question on which to write. I ran through my past mental list of questions. None of these ponderings came with any real inspiration or passion. I experienced no real connection to my questions of the past. Writing requires connection for me. After all, I didn't want to just throw out a question. I wanted to write with wit, wisdom, and great insight. I wanted the reader to chuckle, get misty-eyed, and be confronted with profound truth, all in the space of four hundred words or less. I will admit it's entirely possible I simply wanted to be Anne Lamott.

Fortunately I caught a glimpse of these vain internal ramblings and whispered "Dear God, I need help in getting myself out of the way." And I again set about the work of zeroing in on that one question about which to write. Time and time again, though, I found my mind had meandered back to the self. Frustrated, I repeatedly asked God, "How do I get myself out of the way in order to make room for what is truly important?"

And so it was, sitting on my front porch on a hot day in July, that enlightenment finally came. I chuckled, got misty-eyed, and was confronted with profound truth. In my quest for inspiration, I had been ignoring the one question most present in my life. The question that had been life's recurring theme over the past several years: How do I lay down my life for that which is greater?

As a mother, how do I remove the self in order for my children to grow in the knowledge that they are God's beloved?

As a wife, how do I place understanding before being understood?

As a teacher, how do I bring my gifts to the classroom, without believing I am in control?

And finally, as God's creation, how do I let Anne Lamott be Anne Lamott... and let me be me?

Why Me, God?

William P. Soetenga

*I*t is simply too far away. It may be just around the corner or across the world, but it is too far away from my experience to really comprehend: People in our world actually go to bed without enough food to sustain them and millions of them, every year, die of starvation. I hurry through the areas close to home that might awaken me to the plight of people in my own city and, though I see the graphic, videotaped pictures of people in Darfur, the Republic of Congo, and Haiti, I cannot grasp the reality of what I am seeing with my own eyes. Some would say that the plight of the majority of the people in the world who live without adequate shelter, water, and food results from political corruption, lack of initiative, or simply being in the wrong place at the worst possible time.

The compelling images of the horrors of war that we see in documentaries and on the evening news remind us of the power of evil, the savagery of war, and the awe-full price paid by innocents and combatants. As was true in the forties, fifties, sixties, seventies, and nineties, United States service men and women are at war, this time in real but surreal places like Iraq and Afghanistan and gold stars are seen once again in the shade-drawn windows of American homes. The estimates of opposition force losses and civilian deaths are staggering. Some would say that the carnage of war can not be avoided because evil must be confronted and defeated.

War has never come near our dwelling, even though evil is on every hand. I cannot recall a single day that I did not have shelter in comfortable ambient temperatures, bountiful water and food, love of home and family, the guidance, support, and affirmation of the church—even though I have had no control over being in the "right" place to receive these blessings. My question is one that is common to many: Why me, Lord? Why have I had the privilege of knowing Christ? Why have I known nothing but "milk and honey" throughout my life? Why have I been sheltered from war, abject poverty, natural disasters, and terrorism? I am no better or worse than billions of people that You, God, have created who have never known anything but terror, hunger, war, and disease. Why me, Lord?

That Heavy Rock Question

Jan Slattery Callen

Okay. I have a problem and am not afraid to admit it. David wants me to write a wonderfully deep, thought-provoking kind of question for God that will make everyone say, "Deep. Too deep for me." I, however, have no such question. The only one I can think of is, "if God is all powerful, could He create a rock even He could not move?" Lame, huh? Besides, what difference would that make anyway?

I suppose it is my upbringing. In the innocent times of the 1950s small-town Sikeston, Missouri, I was taught that God has it all under control. His job is to make sure that the forces of nature keep working, and our job is to have faith that it will. Faith that God loves us. It's that whole tapestry image. You know, where we see only the underside. At such a young age, I barely knew what a tapestry was, but I could picture that the underside was surely a mess.

Now I am not naïve enough to think that everything is perfect. Far from it. Ice caps are melting, the ozone is depleting, and entire countries in Africa are dying from AIDS. I also know that these are problems we have created for ourselves and that God is probably sitting up there, shaking His head, feeling bad about the situation. Who can blame him? I feel bad too. But to ask God questions like, "how is this fair" and "why is that right," just seems as if we are saying to Him that we don't trust Him. After all, He put us here in the first place, and we are riding on His ticket to a destination that He has prepared for us. We don't deserve it and didn't ask for it, but we all are blessed with the ride anyway.

You'd think I could ask a question like, "Why did my parents have to die long before I really got to appreciate them?" or "Why did the first man I really loved have to die suddenly at fifty?" These questions are personal and in the real scheme of things don't matter much to anybody but me. I also imagine that when I do get into God's presence I will be so tongue-tied I won't be able to say anything anyway. I will probably just be happy I am there instead of somewhere else.

So, I will stick to that really heavy rock question. Sorry, David. That's all I've got!

Honest with God

Donald D. Johnson

I remember well one scene out of my experience as a pastor when God was called "on the carpet!" A very prominent churchman underwent aggressive cardiac evaluation and ended up having a couple of arteries expanded by the insertion of devises which would remain permanently in place—put there to hold his arteries open. I think we non-medical professionals called this the "balloon treatment." We heaved a collective sigh. He was now, with this new procedure, surely on the mend.

As a matter of fact, it seemed my colleague in ministry would be able with his regained energy to finish the book he was working on and for which his publisher and church were anxiously waiting. He was young by today's standard with life in retirement ahead of him. Certainly it was thought that out of his life in the pulpit and in the classroom he was on the cusp of putting his experience and wisdom to paper in several more articles and books.

It was then he died! I have relived this scene over and over again in similar situations where death has been encountered. But here for me was the purest challenge to an all-powerful God I had ever heard or witnessed. As many of my former seminary professor's closest friends gathered at his home, all of us were trying to speak words of condolence and comfort to his widow. We were all shocked! His death was so unexpected! It seemed so unfair! Out of the silence of the gathering, each of us trying to deal with our own grief, a dear and trusted colleague wailed, "God, You really goofed on this one. When I join John, You are going to have to deal with me. How could You let this happen?" Oddly the outburst did not seem to be out of place. I think we all felt in sympathy with what was said. I know I wished I could have been this honest with God, as had my friend.

I've come to believe such outspoken honesty was possible only out of a very close relationship with the Almighty One. To be able to question God and to do so in the midst of life, in the crucible of pain and anger, is unspeakably wonderful and freeing. To know—to really know that God not only allows us this freedom, but welcomes it is divine healing at its best.

Why Can't We All Get Along?

Dondeena Fleenor Caldwell

Remember the pictures of the riots that took place in Los Angeles in 1991? In one scene the white policemen were beating Rodney King with clubs, a bleeding black man who cried out, "Why can't we all just get along?" Yes, that is the question.

We say that every human being on this earth is created in God's image, yet that image is made up of so many varieties of color, sizes, shapes, languages, customs, beliefs, and talents. If we accept the fact that God created diversity, why, if we are all part of the same world, do we lambast, find fault, criticize, and even kill each other because of our differences? Could it be that I believe my uniqueness alone reflects God's image and is the only true reflection of the divine pattern? Are those who are not quite like me, even the near approximations to "God's image," to be classified as inferior reflections, even abominations—and therefore merit criticism, censure, even persecution?

Why, God, do our differences erupt into criticism, ostracism, even annihilation? Why can't those who profess to love God and claim to be following the teachings found in their holy books get along? Such differences have not always bred division or derision. For seven hundred years the Muslims, Christians, and Jews lived together in Spain as good neighbors. In Seville a Catholic king invited a Moorish (Muslim) architect to design and build the cathedral in which to worship. The building included a minaret to which the Catholics added a bell tower that included a ramp to enable the blind muezzin to ride his donkey to the top to call the faithful Muslims to prayer.

The main entrance to the huge cathedral was a large keyhole arch (Moorish) through which both groups went to worship. "We are going to the mosque for mass," the Catholics said, with no animosity. Both groups used the same building for a hundred and fifty years until an earthquake destroyed much of it.

Rosemary Radford Ruether says in *Disputed Questions*, "To impose one religion on everyone flattens and impoverishes the wealth of human interaction with God, much as imposing one language on everyone steals other people's culture and memories."

Why then, God, do we choose to live with tunnel vision and deride and belittle anyone who looks, acts, feels, or believes differently than we do? Why can't we just get along?

My Question

Sam Bruce

*I*n 1998 we discovered that my wife Sandie had a larger-than-my-fist-size benign brain tumor that blinded her right eye and impaired the left eye. After the tumor was removed, her neurosurgeon was surprised with the results. She exited surgery into a week-long coma that doctors feared she would not return from. When she awoke from the coma, she was like a newborn baby.

Although her memory was intact, she had to relearn everything else: talking, eating, showering, dressing, literally everything. In the church where we had pastored she was an outstanding ministry leader and excellent Bible teacher. She was director of admissions for Wesley College where I was president. She could have been selected Wife and Mother of the Year. Now she started over on a *clean slate*!

I was taught no matter what happens, you don't ask God, "Why?" But on that night, after the neuro-ophthalmologist showed me the MRI, I asked God, "Why?" The most godly, loving, caring, creative woman. Why her?

As I repeatedly asked God my *Why Question* over the next several months, I discovered it didn't shake Him! He enabled me to turn it into a "What Question" Lord, what do You want to do through Sandie's and my lives in this situation?" My e-mail list grew to hundreds as people around the world prayed for her. Her recovery across the past ten years has been slow, yet steady. Her doctors say, "The Lord has indeed touched you. You are a miracle lady! We never dreamed you'd come back this far; you're a testimony to God's healing power!"

Following surgery, Sandie began singing in our concerts, although talking very little; and sharing testimonies of God's healing power. Across the past ten years, we've performed our program *How God Helps Us in the Dark Nights of Life* in eighteen states and fourteen denominations. Following her testimony and singing "Lord of the Troubled Sea" (the song that brought her back to reality!), she regularly receives standing ovations from audiences deeply touched by her praise for "The Lord who is her Healer!"

Our incredible God is still answering our "Why" and "what" questions in amazing ways that boggle minds and bring hope and healing. We understand the truth of Micah 7:8: *Do not gloat over me, my enemy! Though I have fallen, I will rise. Though I sit in darkness, the Lord will be my light.*

Sandie is still *rising* a blessing to everyone who meets her. Some miracles just take a little longer! To God be the glory!

Living in the Questions

Kathleen Davey Buehler

When I was growing up, one of our neighbors across the street was a young woman with two young children. A native of a European country, she was trying to make it on her own in this place so far from her home. My mother became her friend and showered love on her and her children. Even though the woman was from another church tradition, she began coming with us to the Church of God. The young woman seemed to be enjoying our fellowship of believers, but one day she stopped coming and went back to her tradition. Our church was too "free" for her. It left her with too many questions.

I've thought about that situation since then. At times when my life questions seem overwhelming, I too have longed for the answers to be spelled out for me. Wouldn't that make life much more comfortable and easy?

Logically, it would seem that the longer one walks with the Lord, the fewer questions there would be. But that hasn't been my experience. Certainly there are some questions I no longer ask, such as, "Does God love me?" God has already gone to extensive lengths to let me know he loves me. I don't ask if God is real or good or faithful. I already know in my heart that he is.

But other questions surface or recur that have no immediate or simple answers. I ask, How is intercessory prayer "effective"? What does it mean to be filled up with the fullness of God? What does it mean to live well? And to die well? What is the purpose of suffering and can I really understand how to grow through it? Why does evil seem to win so many battles?

The life of faith, I've discovered, is a life of questions. It's part of living out a relationship, rather than a religion. Questions allow for ongoing dialogue with and deeper knowledge of the God of the universe.

I might not always enjoy living in and with the questions. But I'm beginning to make peace with them, to recognize that they are a positive part of this journey where my finite mind meets with that of the infinite God. I'm living with *the* answer in the midst of my questions. And that makes all the difference.

What about My Friends?

Daniel C. Harman

*S*ome words from my mom, shared with a tear so many years ago, come back to me, Father. Maybe You can help me. Over and over, she would say with a sign, "Oh, God, what can I do? My sisters are not Christians, and Lord, You know, they are dear women, real friends. They're too good for the devil, but not good enough for heaven."

Mom's gone now, but her words haunt me. I think of so many people I do love dearly; friends I depend on; friends who love and care for me. But, Lord, they're friends who just don't know Jesus. My question is simple: How can I be happy in heaven if I know these friends haven't made it?

The Bible is full of people who seemed like wonderful people, but there's no record of their actually believing in Christ. The rich young ruler, perhaps, came to himself and returned to Jesus. But we don't know. Pilate's wife pled for Jesus' life, but the Gospels do not tell us of her spiritual condition. Surely Mary, Martha, and Lazarus were true disciples, but with Jesus' mild rebuke of Martha, should we assume she wasn't a believer? She served the master great food, we are sure, but what of her soul?

And, Oh my! My own family—some are lost—friends, neighbors, business acquaintances, friends I have studied with. They're wonderful, but so few know Jesus.

And today, there are so many good people in the world. So many crusades for marvelous, people-helping causes. People we're proud to have leading the wide variety of humanitarian efforts. They're people I'd love to meet in heaven, but will I see them up there? Tell me, Lord, can I be happy if I don't?

There are, of course, so many godly people I am anxious to see once more over on the other side: dear saints, skilled Christian leaders, and church members from a dozen branches of the family of God. Oh, what a joyful, blessed reunion that will be. I, for one, am glad there's an eternity for me to roam about and enjoy great fellowship.

But will my joy be limited? Will my heavenly happiness be curtailed? Please, Lord, when you have a minute, give me some answers. Thank you.

How Soon Will Jesus Return?

Norma Massie Armogum

My mother recently died and went home to be with You. I miss her and look forward to seeing her again. There will be great rejoicing when we are reunited. Surely she will greet me and show me around heaven when I arrive.

Going through the grieving of my recent loss causes me to ponder heaven and what Mom is experiencing there. Surely she is singing with the angels, dancing with joy, and talking with old and new friends. Maybe she has a garden where she tends her roses and sometimes sits to write poetry. I know she must spend time worshiping You because she loved You so much while she was here on earth.

God, what is heaven really like? The Bible describes it as a glorious place. It is said to be a place where there is no sorrow, no crying, no hurting, and no pain. (Revelation 21:4) Surely it is a place where there is no evil, no hunger, and no longing for anything.

When I think of heaven I think about the awesome glory of God surrounding everything, shining brilliantly as the source of light. People there are always happy, filled with great joy, smiling and laughing with one another. I see heaven as a place where mighty angels come and go according to the work God has assigned them.

The beauty of heaven must be breathtaking. Revelation 21 talks about streets made of pure gold and of gates made of pearl. When I consider this I think of sights, sounds, smells, and tastes that no one has ever experienced here on earth. God, as people on earth pray, can one really see their prayers rising as incense to Your throne? (Psalm 141:2 and Revelation 8:3-4)

What peace and joy, what sense of fulfillment there must be in heaven. How can anyone think of this wonderful place and not want to be there?

So, God, when will Jesus return? How soon will we be able to enjoy heaven with You? I don't long for it as one who is grieving the loss of a loved one. Nor do I long for heaven as one who is tired of living on earth. I look forward to heaven as some time in the future, when my well-lived life on earth is done and when I'm ready to rest in your presence. Lord, when will that time come? Although I look forward to it, I don't want it to be too soon. I have loved ones who don't know You yet and before You come I want them to be ready to meet You.

Impartial, God?

Donald L. Allbaugh

*H*ello, God? Thanks for taking my call. Love Your show. Long time listener, first time caller. While I was on hold I heard some questions that I wonder about too; why the innocent suffer, why injustice so often triumphs, why evildoers go un-punished. Your answers didn't clear everything up for me, but then I plan to keep listening to Your program until all those knotty little conundrums are explained.

What I really don't understand is how You can bestow perfect and uninterrupted love to every single one of Your creatures. Luke tells us that You are *no respecter of persons.* To me that means that Your love is extended to the just and the unjust in equal measure and is, in no way, contingent on our worthiness. Complete devotion to a few I completely get. When I first glimpsed my newborn children, I was bound to them with bands of steel forged in the white-hot crucible of my soul. Seeing some small part of me reflected in their upturned faces reminded me that I am made in Your image.

Do You see Your reflection when You look at me? I shrink from that thought. It both intrigues and astounds me. A spark of divinity flickering ever so faintly from this fallible mortal? What does burn within me is the implausibility that I could love someone who would deliberately harm my child. How can You love perfectly both a grievously wounded abuse victim and her calloused victimizer?

Since I provide court-ordered therapy to sex offenders, I spend some days listening to myriad excuses for indefensible behavior. At such times I have the impulse to compile a list of those who seem wholly undeserving of Your love. How much safer would the lives of battered women and sexual abuse victims be if their tormentors were not in their lives. Some offenders betray not the slightest hint of compassion or concern for anyone but themselves. But then I peer, aghast, into the dark crevasses where my own character defects slither. At such times of introspective clarity I am overwhelmed by Your grace and yearn, perhaps in some small way as You do, that all might bask in its redeeming radiance.

Still, though, Your thoughts about all of this would be very much appreciated. Again, thanks for taking my call. I won't tie up the phone lines any longer. I'll take my answer off the air.

Wandering and Wondering

Leslie H. Mosier

oday I applied for social security benefits at age sixty-two. Driving to my appointment some nagging thoughts crept to center stage in my mind. "Where did the years go? How has it all slipped away so quickly? I wish life offered a backspace key to erase dumb mistakes and allow do-overs."

You can see where this is going. Regrets turned to accusations. As a Christian I've always believed that God guides one's life journey. So, why did He allow me to make some bonehead decisions that surely couldn't have been His will for me. Missed opportunities.

Wasted potential. Wrong direction. Lord, I know I'm not your puppet, but why on earth did You allow my foolish detours to impede your ultimate plan, for my life? With a little nudge then and there we could have done great things together!

Over the past few days I've done some soul-searching about destiny, free will, life plans, and such. It's been a reassuring reminder that while we offer the Creator lemons, He is still in the business of making lemonade. My faith journey assures me that we can trust God to do what's right. He will not abandon us. His promise to Jacob still rings true for every believer. *I am with you and will watch over you wherever you go* —Genesis 28:15.

Amazingly, scripture assures us that imperfect people of faith are part of *the overall purpose he is working out in everything and everyone* —Ephesians 1:11 MSG. Even more startling is Paul's affirmation, *We know that God causes everything to work together for the good of those who love God and are called according to his purpose for them* —Romans 8:28 NLT. Apparently, there is no waste in God's workshop.

We all have regrets. That's part of being human. Watching my ten-month-old grandson, Logan, I'm reminded that we begin as helpless babies and grow to adulthood drooling, stumbling, trying, failing, succeeding, falling, but always getting back up to try again. Through the years God watches, encourages, and helps put the "Humpty-Dumpty" pieces back together when we break. Though we may stray, He will stay. Peter echoed this thought when he wrote, *Let Him have all your worries and cares, for He is always thinking about you and watching everything that concerns you* —I Peter 5:7. Through all my wandering and wondering, I find myself returning to this fundamental conviction. Life is full of uncertainty, but when we find answers to the big questions of eternity, all the little questions of this brief existence fall into perspective.

Someone Had to Ask

Jack W. Williams

"There lives more faith in honest doubt than in half the creeds," wrote Mr. Tennyson.

And so, Lord of Lords, King of Kings, I ask: How is it You can watch one of them glide safely into the Hudson with a picture perfect splash and the other one pitch, roll, plunge, and explode into a fiery inferno? Would You have allowed Your Son to be on the cover of a bestseller flashing a televangelist's grin? How can a God so big stay so well hid? Hey, are those my prayers caught up there on the cover of the flue (Surely He sees me down on my knees)? Why would a sovereign and just God be hung up on glory, honor, power, and praise? Would He be grieved to know I'm writing a book with the working title, *The Practice of the Absence of God?* Or relieved to know I have writer's block? Though You slay me, am I to trust You? By the way, Father, where is the Lamb? But, honestly, don't I idolize and deify You because of what's in it for me? Have You ever thought of using ecstasy instead of suffering (How odd of God to use the blues)? What if I just have the faith of a mustard packet? Why do bad things happen to good people—assuming, of course, that I'm good people? Which one am I, O God, the priest, the Levite, or the Samaritan? Can't a man take a sick day after a dark night of the soul? How long will we feel the tease of the transcendent? Does a half flicker of hope in a human heart count for ironclad revelation? Why am I a diabetic with an insulin addiction? Why did you make me thus? Does my ancient foe really seek to work me woe? Why am I embarrassed to talk about my ancient foe? Didn't I read your obituary in *Time* magazine back in the 1960s? Do we have to believe in freewill? Do we have a choice? Isn't the law of averages the same as predestination? Any chance I could get a little more face time with You? Any chance I could get more face time—and live to tell? Is there hope for a misanthrope? Mercy for a misbeliever? On this altar, I rest a fresh bouquet of qualms.

Faithful Uncertainty

Richard L. Willowby

Not long ago, the late Dr. George Kufeldt and I were talking about the tragedies and struggles we have encountered in life. Dr. Kufeldt buried three wives. I have encountered a few soul-wrenching tragedies as well. We discussed the grace of God in such times, the pain of loss, and the difficulty of recovery. Neither of us asked why. We had already asked that question many times. Instead, we focused on the steadfast love of God and loving support of God's people and even people unrelated to church who expressed concern and offered genuine help.

Across my more then thirty years of ministry, the "why" question has often appeared. I understand the question and the need to ask it. I've stood beside the casket and the open grave of a child. Why? His mother asks. Whatever the answer may be: What is remains. The child is dead.

Often people have told me that they are "learning to live with the questions," like that in itself provided the answer, but few explain what that might mean. Learning to live amid important questions with authentic faith challenges me. I do not desire a faith where questions are swept under the mental rug, or reality is reinterpreted to fit one's theology. What is remains. The child is dead.

Worse, some know. They frighten me. Accusing and condemning, they abuse others with their superior knowledge. Through them the oppressive spirit of the Pharisees lives in our time. Such thinking leads to a Waco standoff, a community drink of poisoned Kool-Aid, a suicide bombing. In our churches it marginalizes those who most need our help and isolates us.

I want to approach great questions (and even the little ones) with a strong dose of humility and compassion. The truth lives through the Living Word, the Christ, the One Who is God with us. He wrestles with us, not against us. The Gospels show a Jesus who prayed over His own questions. He struggled with His ultimate question in the Garden of Gethsemane. Can we expect a different road?

It is enough—more than enough—to face life's questions head on and struggle for answers; Yes. But beyond answers is honest faith in the One Who walks with us, day in and day out in loving companionship. *Knowledge puffs up, but love builds up. Anyone who claims to know something does not yet have the necessary knowledge; but anyone who loves God is known by him* —1 Corinthians 8:1b-3 NRSV.

What Really Happened?

John M. Johnson

I was teaching Introduction to Theology to Lebanese, Syrian, and Jordanian students during my first year at Mediterranean Bible College in Beirut, Lebanon. The course calendar was centered on Christology and the yearly calendar was pushing us toward Holy Week. Hence the question: "What happened on the cross?" I was looking for a conversation about redemption and reconciliation.

We searched the biblical record, shared testimonies and got comfortable with "theological talk." It was a good class. Toward the end of the session one young woman raised her hand and asked, "What really happened on the cross?" I gave a recap, thinking the conversation that day had somehow passed over her head. Perhaps she hadn't been listening.

As I finished my summary she posed the question in a new way. "You said that God was in Jesus Christ and that Jesus Christ was one hundred percent God and one hundred percent man, right?" I nodded my head. "You said that Jesus died on the cross to redeem us all, right?" "Yes," I said. "So, did God die on the cross?" she queried.

Doing what any good teacher will do when confronted with a really good question, I stalled. "What do you think? Did God die on the cross?" gesturing to the entire class. More conversation. Again the young woman pushed the question in my direction.

"For me, it is a mystery. I cannot explain the details of the cross event. I believe it happened in history. I believe that Jesus' death on the cross has reconciled me to God. I believe that Jesus is the atoning sacrifice for the world if people will but accept it." The bell rang and class ended. "We'll talk about this more next time," I said, as the students exited.

My "it is a mystery" answer didn't really satisfy the student nor had it satisfied me. I passed by Dr. Fouad Melki's office. "Do you have a moment? I would like to ask a question." He waved me in with a friendly smile.

Dr. Melki listened as I told him of the class, the conversation, and the final question. He also listened to my answer. And then he shared his thoughts. "To understand what happened on the cross, you have to understand the nature of death. Death," he continued, "is not passing out of existence." And it began to come into focus, this mystery.

My question for God? What really happened on the cross?

Questions First!

Judy Spencer Nelon

Asking questions is something I have always felt comfortable doing. Being raised in a strict family with a lot of "nos" certainly caused me to often question "why not." My loving family atmosphere made me feel safe with my often-asked questions.

One of the most important things I teach the people who work with me is to never be afraid to ask too many questions. It is important to make sure one understands what is expected in any situation. I have found the best way to get good results is from making sure all the questions have been asked. One of my all-time favorite scriptures is:

Keep asking, and it will be given to you —Matthew 7:7 ISV.

My husband Rex Nelon and I had only been married a short time when he asked me why I responded to his questions with another question and not the expected answer. I explained that I needed more information to answer his questions. He thought that was actually pretty smart and we enjoyed a good laugh together. Rex and I had married as adults, older with children and grandchildren. Life experiences have taught me to get all the facts before I answer too quickly any question asked.

On the other hand sometimes we get too confident and don't ask the questions often enough. If I had to pinpoint any one thing that has lead to events in my life that I regret, it would be the times I did not ask more questions to make better judgments and decisions. My quiet smart ninety years of age momma normally stayed out of her family's business, but I'll always remember when she boldly told me not to buy a thirtieth floor condo. I had paid a pre-construction deposit planning to sell it quickly for a profit. I attributed her obvious fear to her age, and chose not to listen to her wise advice. How would she know the economy was about to collapse in the United States? I completed the purchase. For the next two years I suffered and prayed. Well, okay I begged God to please rescue me from the disaster that looked as if it would be my financial ruin. A decorator friend helped me make it amazingly beautiful. It was featured on HGTV and still no sale. After much prayer and serious spiritual growth, the place sold. Now I ask first!

Who Are You?

Norman E. Beard

At first this appeared to be an easy topic. Five drafts and one hundred questions later it seemed impossible. Many focus on their own concept of God and His work. I discovered a glut of available information. There is the World Wide Web, books, television, lessons, lectures, and sermons from teachers, learned professors, ministers, family, and friends. However I found most of the data unclear, confusing, and often contradictory. There is a wide variety of knowledge from all over the world.

Here are some personal and practical questions that I have been reluctant to ask. Are You male or female? Or some other gender-neutral being? Where do You live? Heaven? Earth? In our hearts or somewhere else? Can You sing or play a musical instrument? What kind of music do You like? Hymns? Spiritual? Country? Jazz? Rock? Do You speak and understand all the world's languages? What language do You speak at home? What Bible version would You recommend? King James? NIV? RSV? NSV? *The New English Bible*, or the *Bible Story Book* by Elsie Egermeier?

I have seen much of the world You have made. It is beautiful. Though different from the Arctic to the Amazon, it is magnificent. Can we learn more about You by seeing the mountains of the Alps and Andes? Consider the Danube River, the Great Barrier Reef, the Sahara Desert, a Norwegian fjord, and myriads of Your grand creations. I see Your handiwork in all that You have made.

When will You reveal the mysteries of God? Are these so different that we may be better off not knowing? Why are there disasters such as storms, hurricanes, tornadoes, floods, and tsunamis? Are there really acts of God or is there some other force to blame? Can You do anything about hunger and poverty while abundance and affluence coexist? Why is there pain, illness, suffering, and death? Will You explain the Trinity? Do You ever disagree? Who is in charge? What do You look like? A Warner Sallman painting?

If I had to narrow it down to one key concept to help us understand, it might be the following: What is Your name? *I am who I am!* Or do You use a nickname? Who are You? Who am I? How can we relate to each other in this world beyond?

A Dialogue with God

Alvin Lewis

*J*t is a humbling experience to have a fifteen minute dialogue with God. Uppermost I want to give thanks for the gift of grace and salvation. It was God's grace and salvation that marked the turning point in my life. Having been born in a state of poverty and reared in an environment of deprivation and desperation, I have been emancipated by Your miraculous grace—a grace that transformed my life from the pits of pity to a life of profound peace.

I remember, dear God, so vividly those early childhood and adolescent years of growing up on Chicago's west side in the forties and fifties. Those were some of the dark days in my life. Poverty was pandemic and opportunities were few. Drugs, alcohol, gambling, and crime abounded on every street corner. So many of my friends became the victims of drugs and crime and died early deaths. And I am still here, but only by your grace. Thank you Father for being my protector. Thank you Jesus for being my Savior. Thank you Holy Spirit for empowering and keeping me saved to do the will of God.

Lord, you have taken me on a joyful journey for over fifty years of graceful living. I have come to this conclusion: I have been given supernatural grace. Your blessings have flowed, from the throne of grace, to the lives of others whom you have allowed to impart gifts of grace and blessings to my life. Therefore, I am grateful that you have allowed my life to intersect with spiritual giants, and servant leaders, known to everyone and others, known only to you. For these significant people, I wish to give thanks.

My wife, Dr. Juanita Lewis, who has been my loving, faithful, and supportive companion for over fifty years, whose gentleness, kindness, and generosity are emblematic of her character. Thank you for our three children: Alvin Vaughn, Lydia Janese, and Lystrelle Daneen who have brought happiness and fulfillment to our lives.

For a mother, Lillie May Harper-Lewis, who taught me the meaning of right and wrong. For my father, Simpson Lewis, who taught how to be responsible and accountable for my actions.

For minister, Della Brown, who preached the gospel and in a cottage prayer meeting invited me to accept Christ; for Claude and Addie Wyatt who nurtured me early in my Christian journey; and for Sethard Beverly who served as a mentor and friend in the formative years of my ministry.

And specials appreciation to Jesus who continues to allow me to walk with Him.

Why Joshua, God?

John L. Albright

I have lots of questions for God; so many I may sound like a whining three-year-old child—whyeee? I suspect I'm not alone in asking this one:

Why, God? Why did Joshua get to go into

the promised land, and not Moses? After all

You chose Moses to lead that long arduous

journey. He did all the hard work, and for

years put up with so much complaining. He

was faithful. It just doesn't seem fair. So

why, God? Why didn't You reward Moses?

Some years ago, at a ministers' conference, I heard the speaker say, "If your dream can be realized in your lifetime, then your dream isn't big enough."

I struggled with that for several weeks, then a scripture came to mind: Paul writes,

I planted the seeds, Apollos watered them,
but God made them sprout and grow. —1 Corinthians 3:6 CEV.

Here's a wise axiom: You can get a lot done if you don't care who gets the credit.

So, like Moses, I do my best, then pass it on. Some of my dreams are realized; some are not. An old gospel song states: "Farther along, we'll know all about it; farther along, we'll understand why..." I trust that from an eternal perspective, God answers our whys.

God made me an inquisitive being. God understands me, and is big enough to accept and deal with my questions and doubts. Because of that, I guess I'll keep asking, and at times, even enjoy it.

Why Me God, Why Me?

David L. Lawson

That is our question when we have been severely disappointed, when we have suffered unalterable frustration, when we have been faced with unspeakable loss and our grief is too much to bear. Like Job of old, we are convinced we have been singled out for hardship no one else endures.

The Psalmist viewed it differently when he asked "What is man that Thou are mindful of him?!" He was asking "Why are You so good to us, God?" Yes, hardships come, but how wonderfully God provides.

I remember such an event in my life. As a young boy, I had joined in many worship experiences as the congregation sang joyfully the hymns of the Church of God. I grew to love those songs and to read about the pioneer servants who had written them. In fact, even yet, when I sing one of those great songs, I think of the people who joined me in singing and their lives and service.

Years later, I traveled as a part of my work in World Service to Kenya, East Africa. I was far from home. I dearly missed my wife and two very little girls. I stood at night looking up at the stars wondering if I was really equipped for work that took me so far from family and home.

One evening, a group of Christian leaders who had been touring various mission stations gathered, and we began singing. Among the travelers was Lawrence Brooks—dedicated, pioneer minister. I was astounded to realize that we were singing a hymn I had sung many times across my life and that the writer of the song was in the circle singing it with me. We sang "He lifted me out of the deep miry clay; He settled my feet in the straight, narrow way; He lifted me up to a heavenly place, And floodeth my soul each day with His grace."

What a moment! My soul was indeed filled with His grace! I had been lifted up! I knew I was experiencing a rich moment I didn't deserve. The hymn was a gospel reminder. The author, Lawrence Brooks, was a Christian model whom I had been privileged to meet and love. Halfway across the world from my home, a blessing I didn't deserve and could not have anticipated was mine.

God generously gave it! Why me, God, why me??

Why Must We Suffer?

Jeffrey K. Lockhart

As a cancer survivor, I admit that I struggled with fear and anxiety following my diagnosis and treatments. I also found it difficult to find "joy" in my life when often it took every ounce of strength I had just to face radiation and chemotherapy. It was difficult to see how any good could come from that suffering. I did ask God ques-tions as to Why Must We Suffer? These are insights He gave to me:

What is the purpose of our suffering here on Earth?

I am not sure why Christians must suffer here on Earth; however, I believe that there is real purpose in our suffering. So, I turned to His Word and promises to find strength, joy, and purpose. I believe I found some purpose for suffering and strife in 2 Corinthians 1:3-11. It is so you can receive comfort from God, therefore being able to provide similar comfort to others; to devote yourself to prayer and to give God the glory He deserves for answering what we ask of Him.

Is it OK to feel fearful and anxious when you are facing a tough time in life?

Since Jesus took on the form of man, He understands our fears and anxieties. He suffered and experienced grief and sorrow. As I walked through the cancer experience, my prayer was that I would see clearly a path laid out for me by God, and be strong enough to walk it. Paul often reminds us there will be suffering here on Earth; but, God will always be with us. If we could adopt Paul's statement from Philippians *to live is Christ*...I believe that facing the struggles of this world would be more of an opportunity to live in the strength of Christ, and to bring glory to Him through suffering.

Why are we supposed to seek "joy" when we are suffering?

During the worst part of my cancer treatments, my feelings and experiences were not so great. Every day I knew that He gave me strength to get out of bed, go through the routine of getting ready, and face what was ahead. Daily I quoted Psalm 118:24; although, I can tell you some days I had trouble believing it. I modified it to say "God, You gave me today, please help me find what it is you want me to rejoice and be glad about." God desires that I trust Him. If for no other reason but the fact that He loves me, I can rejoice and be glad in that.

"Does God Know My Name?"

Fredrick H. Shively

As I pondered questions for God, my mind went back to a moment when Kevin, our older son, was five years old. It happened at night when I was putting him to bed. After we prayed, he asked a question that I had never been asked before: "Daddy, is it too late to get your name in the Bible?"

I replied, "Kevin, the Bible has already been written." Not to be stopped, Kevin followed, "What about the New Testament?" I wondered why he would ask such a question. Then I realized that Kevin Fredrick could find neither of his names there, while his little brother, Mark Jonathan, had names from both the Old and New Testaments.

I wish that I had been as wise in that moment as I was later. I went back to Kevin to say, "Son, although it is not spelled exactly as we spell it, your name is in the Bible. It is on every page. The Bible was written with you in mind. When John 3:16 states, *For God so loved...*, put your name there. Every time you read in the Scriptures, *whoever* or *If anyone would...*, you are there." The miracle of the gospel of God is that it speaks to real human concerns and is addressed to every person who lives.

Names have great significance in the Scriptures because they represent real persons whose stories teach us about ourselves. We identify with them: Abraham on a great quest, Isaiah with a call to speak to the people, Ruth who loses her husband and finds new love, Peter who finds that he is taking on challenges he had never anticipated, Mary Magdalene whose life is dramatically changed. These names become paradigms of our own experiences. We are there—our concerns, our fears, our hopes, our questions. It is no mere coincidence that the gospel speaks about us and to us.

Perhaps we can translate Kevin's question into "Do I matter to You, God?" In a world of teeming masses and growing anonymity, can we say that each one of us has a place at the table of life, with our own nameplate? As with Kevin's question, the answer is "Yes." The message of the Scriptures is that God knows each of us and loves us beyond measure.

I am grateful for Kevin's question that I believe is a question from all of us to God.

What Has Become of Our Loved Ones?

David E. Markle

This chapter in my life brings a heightened curiosity about those who have died. Some years ago, a widow asked me this question again and again after the death of her husband. Frankly, I became annoyed with her. I thought that my biblically-sound responses should quiet her concern. She was not satisfied. I had experienced the deaths of all four of my grandparents, some aunts and uncles, a couple of friends in Vietnam. My answers up to then had always sufficed. Then my sister died at the age of fifty. A year later, a near cousin, also younger than me, died suddenly. Now, I understand her concern more clearly. Before it was only her question, now it is mine, too. What has become of our loved ones who have died and what are they now doing?

The heart of the biblical answer is that they are with Jesus. That may not be as serene as it sounded when I was a child. Jesus took the greatest risk ever in coming here as one of us to serve sacrificially, to speak truth to us about living, and to die for us to make the way for our reconciliation with God. This ministry of reconciliation that Jesus launched on Earth has "all things" in the cosmos in view. Perhaps we get a foretaste of it in what Madeleine L'Engle described as "the hour of love...when God's creature, time, and God's human creatures, like us, collaborate with each other" (*Glimpses of Grace*, 20).

Work is God's good gift to us "pre-Fall" and one might make the case that God will have lots of good, soul-satisfying work for His children in the age to come, without the "drag" of "thorns" and "sweat of the brow" or any other consequence of our wandering into "our own way." This is the ultimate adventure! So, I have a hard time believing that our Lord is preparing "tea and crumpets" for us in the hereafter. Adventure, yes—a real feast of fellowship, soul health, service, and worship with all the peoples of Earth!

Even in this partial answer mystery remains. At home with mystery we find ourselves in good company. The apostle John witnessed: *Beloved, we are God's children now; what we will be has not yet been revealed. What we do know is this: when he is revealed, we will be like him, for we will see him as he is. And all who have this hope in him purify themselves, just as he is pure* —1 John 3:2-3 NRSV.

Ask the Supreme CEO

Charles R. Shumate

ookie crumbs. Lego pieces all over the floor. Balloons floating in the air. Toy trucks zooming across the rug. Sponge Bob Macaroni followed by s'mores around the campfire. The five grand-kids at the lake for a week. What excitement! I can hardly sleep.

One evening around the campfire, after a full day of skiing, I invited the grandchildren to close their eyes and imagine they were standing before God and could ask him anything. The notion was not to ask for anything, but to ask anything they would like to know from the supreme CEO (Created Everything Officer). Addison said, "Why did the dinosaurs become extinct?" Louis commented, "How did you create the world?" Chase added, "Why is there so much evil in the world?" And then Bella shouted, "I would jump on His lap and give Him a big fat hug." I'm amazed they didn't ask "Is there a McDonalds in heaven?" because they love Chicken McNuggets. These are simple questions, but ones we might ask, too. My curiosity would pose the same thoughts, including some hows and whys.

The lyric of a song says, "There's a place where tears don't cry and hearts don't break. We'll never ever wonder 'why' again. The questions here, He will answer there, where tears don't cry and hearts don't break." However, is there a nagging question I would like to ask God now? Yes. Asking God a question for understanding depends on where you are in life and your understanding of who God is. Some may see God as an ogre sitting in heaven causing us to squirm like worms in the hot ashes of life. They might wonder why God would allow killing, war, hatred, and starvation. Why would God allow cancer and AIDS? If a person is in a relationship with God he or she might say, "Why would You love me so?" Now, that's a real question that requires deep reflection about the cross and grace and justice.

Questions are good. They lead to information and understanding. If you could ask God anything, what would it be? I would ask God something such as who really shot Kennedy? Or what words did Jesus yell out when He hit His thumb with a hammer while driving a nail? Another question: Do You get tired of hearing all our whining and complaining? Why is life so complicated?

However, a more appropriate question would be why we are here. And what is the meaning of life? You created all things and invite us to be involved in Your world. You love to be involved in our lives and yet You give us free will. God, You are depending upon us to use our influence to make this world a better place. We are working on it.

Why Did It Take So Long?

D. Dewayne Repass

*W*hy did it take me so long...to discover that prayer was not talking to You but really was communicating with You? Forgive me for being satisfied with an elementary relationship when what You had in mind was a companionship. Thank You for a prayer journey that led to discovering a welcome, open, candid conversation with a personal God.

Why did it take me so long...to stop asking You "why questions" and begin walking with You into answers. Pardon me for my selfish and simplistic approach to religion. The search for a four leaf clover or lucky horseshoes reminds me of attempts to knock Your door down with WHY? questions. While I can't lay claim to much divine revelation, I've often enjoyed moments of rapt awe and what others have referenced as mystery. Thank You for times of sacred silence and serendipitous wisdom.

Why did it take me so long...to understand the Lordship of Christ's beckoning invitation to leave behind the "letter of the law" and to value the "Spirit of the law?" I'm ashamed of confrontational moments when I've had a stone to hurl or some point to prove. Perhaps what You wrote in the dust kneeling before a condemned woman were names like mine whom You have also forgiven.

Why did it take me so long...to trust that the Bible means what it means, not what it says? Don't get me wrong—I'm really grateful for my childhood Sunday school years. My brain cells are full of scriptural stories and KJV verses (thanks, Mrs. Johnson). Father, thank You for freeing me from the shackles of biased truth and opening me up to the Spirit's counsel.

Just one more thing, Lord....

What's with this diabetes thing? It's been thirty years and 30,549 needle injections—and based upon my life expectancy—14,600 more to come. I've told stories of Your saving hand upon my life when sugar levels were as low as the floor of the Grand Canyon and as high as the summit of Mount Everest. Dr. Alexander, my endocrinologist, (he often reminds me of You) once remarked that I need not wait on Your healing touch to bring life back into my pancreas. Receive my thanks again today for a faith journey that reveals Your miracle in a vial of insulin that promises me a tomorrow!

When There Is No Need for Faith and Hope

William A. White

A revelation (insight, perhaps) happened one morning recently that came to me quite unexpectedly as two thoughts merged together. It's possible that someone has already thought of this but I hadn't read or heard about it, until that eventful morning.

I was in my truck on the way to a golf course to play some golf with some friends. I need to tell you that when I'm alone in my truck I often sense a feeling that I'm in a sanctuary, my personal sanctuary, and find that worshiping God and praying come naturally to me there.

This experience happened on a Monday at 7:30 am. Some background may help. Just before leaving to play, I was working on a writing assignment for the Committee on Uniform Series (a committee of the National Council of Churches). The assignment had to do with Jesus Christ's expected Advent, also known as the Second Coming or the Parousia or the Day of the Lord or the expected coming of the Lord from heaven to gather those who have fallen asleep and those still alive to meet in the air to be with him forever, as recorded in 1 Thessalonians. So the thoughts of meeting God face to face and heaven were on my mind.

On that day I was praying (with my eyes wide-open, by the way) and the thought occurred to me to just stop verbalizing for a moment and listen. As I paused to do that, I felt sense of calm and I waited. After few moments, I heard no voice, but I thought of Paul's love chapter and particularly the words at the end: *And now these three remain: faith, hope and love. But the greatest of these is love* – 1 Corinthians 13:1-13. A question came to mind: Why is love greater than faith and hope? The answer that popped into my mind was the following: It's because once we have been caught up in the clouds to meet the Lord in the air to be with the Lord forever, there will be no need for faith and hope. If heaven is anything it is where love is, God's love, agape love. As believers in Christ, we will inherit an eternal dwelling not made with human hands, which we now hope for and have faith in, but then we will "see." (2 Corinthians 5:1-11)

I'm not a theologian but what I experienced made sense to me then, as it does to me now.

How Can We Understand Scripture Faithfully?

Nathan J. Willowby

hortly after my niece began talking, I remember watching her repeatedly ask, "What you say, Papa?" As I imagine the glorious opportunity to spend fifteen minutes with God, I might ask too many questions and not stop to hear God's response. We would be better off briefly stating, "What you say, Papa?" and listening to the clarification of what God has shared with us both through Jesus and Scripture, but that we haven't understood.

I have many questions. Why Abram? Why not Asia? Why the Bible? Why so many churches? Why Mary? But more specifically, I wonder how we should understand, use, and respond to God's teachings in the Bible?

We ask, "What you say, Papa?" and hope that we understand and respond faithfully to what God has said for thousands of years. We go to the Bible, hoping to understand what it means to be God's people in certain circumstances and contexts. Part of the challenge as we dig in and try to follow God, is that even in the Bible, God's people don't always follow God's instructions. God gives the Ten Commandments to Moses, yet the people grow restless and make their own *golden calf,* breaking God's command concerning idols. Then, the prophets have to repeatedly call Israel back to faithfulness. Ephesians 4 calls for unity of the body of Christ, yet there remains strife and division among Christian churches both in the New Testament and today.

So God, how can we approach Your Word most fruitfully and faithfully? Perhaps we should read the Bible thinking we don't know what each passage is about. What if we read the story of the flood with new eyes and looked at all the little details to see what we may have missed? What if we truly approached the Bible believing that God is truly speaking and we will learn something new in every reading? We could read expecting a fresh word that doesn't box the Holy Spirit into certain expectations. Dietrich Bonhoeffer offers one answer, "We will only be happy in our reading of the Bible when we dare to approach it as the means by which God really speaks to us, the God who loves us and will not leave us with our questions unanswered." In this way, we find ourselves at a place where our questions lead us to realize that perhaps God has already answered and if we can listen, we will see in God's Word exactly how we are to faithfully respond.

Loud and Clear?

Kenneth F. Hall

*I*n a dream I wandered, lost all night through the endless streets and alleys of an immense, dark city. I was tired and hungry and confused. At last I seemed to rouse myself just a bit and looked up to where I thought God would be. "Why don't You tell me in plain, clear words just how to get out of here?"

I tried to tell the Lord what I had been experiencing. There was the policeman who seemed too busy directing traffic to speak to me. I had followed one promising road for miles until it led me to the end of a wharf in a dirty harbor. I had even looked in the pocket Testament I carried. But the day was dark, the type was small, and the first sentence I read seemed to have nothing to do with my situation.

I felt the Lord's kindness and concern, but I did not hear an answer. Yet, having looked to the Lord, I huddled back under my covers, and my dream rolled on.

If anything I grew more tired as I walked, but the day seemed a bit brighter. Now my eyes and ears opened to the sordid world I had found myself trapped in. I almost stumbled over an old woman waiting to cross the street, and for once I paused long enough to help her. She thanked me and even asked what I was doing in that part of town. It turned out that she had a small idea about a way to leave the city. I walked on and was tempted to give up on her suggestion, but patience came. A church that had looked forbidding at first drew me to its doors where I found shelter and prayed. Soon a group of children burst through the doors and dashed for a bus stop down the street. I was drawn along by their laughter and friendly chatter. I could trust that bus to take me where I needed to go. My heart reached out to a world around me that now made sense.

Finally as I looked toward my bedroom window, the dawn started to break. Had the Lord been speaking to me? I knew that sometimes God does call in a clear voice. Sometimes that comes through His Word. But this time God might be looking for me to learn from an open-hearted search that would expose me to His world, to His people, and to His ways.

Thanks for Listening

Sharon Cook Harrison

As I was lying leisurely in my hammock enjoying the beautiful blue sky with white fluffy clouds, I began to think about non-important but unanswered questions I have. So Father, perhaps you could answer a few of these.

First of all, I thank you for the relationship that I have with You. I am in awe that You loved me so much that You made Yourself known to me when I was very young. Never have You left me nor loved me less.

So for my first question. You said that the very hairs of one's head are numbered. How in the world can You know that? How can You keep track? Even if I was counting I wouldn't know where to begin with my own head let alone everyone else's. Was this a statement just to let us know how much You do care for us? Would people's baldness help You out?

There's a saying "which comes first, the chicken or the egg?" I realize this is not in scripture, so is the right answer the chicken since I don't remember You saying on such or such a day You created the egg?

Since the eagle teaches its eaglet how to fly, who taught the eagle? When You created the eagle did You also instruct it on what to do with its offspring? By the way, how the eagle pushes its little one out of the nest and then flies down beneath it and catches it on its wing is such a beautiful illustration of how You are there to catch us.

In the first chapter of Genesis You tell us what you created in six days. Then all the heavens and the earth and all the host of them were finished. So on the seventh day You rested from all of Your work. How did You rest? Did You just lie back and enjoy what You had created? It must have been an awesome day for you. Was it hard to go back to work on Monday? I am sure we could all learn to rest better if we knew what You did.

It is said that we humans only use a small percentage of our brains. Some of us probably tip the scale way down. Since You are smarter than any of us, how can we make better use of what You have given us? I hope I use enough of my brain to show what is really in my heart.

Thanks Father for listening.

The Origin of God

Mick Gilliam

t first I was dismayed. I asked those in my inner circle what they would ask God if they had a one-on-one chat with the Almighty. I heard "Is there a literal hell?" or "Do dogs go to heaven?"

After wrestling with several points of inquiry, I had to face the question that has for decades given me fits. God, where do You come from? Where is Your point of origin? Did someone create You? This makes my brain literally hurt. I can feel my gray matter convulsing inside my cranium.

Now, of course, I know the conventional answers from systematic theologies that teach us that God is self-existent and eternal. He is the universal cosmic alpha and omega. There is none like Him. Okay. I believe that. Maybe I should leave the grander mysteries for greater minds to ponder... Or for God alone to know. After all, His ways are higher and transcendent—far beyond the scope and understanding of the mind of man.

God's story commences with "In the beginning God created the heavens and the earth:" Do you see? No mention of His background? Did He come from a family of happy mommy and daddy Gods? Did they have first names like Jehovah, Elohim, El Shaddai, Adonai?

Scripture gives us subtle hints about God's celestial habitations. But there is no concrete illustration of His origin. I have reflected on the various deities of religions outside the Judeo-Christian stream and some of their narratives depict their birth. I am glad that my God is nothing like the capricious characters in the Roman and Greek pantheons. I also take great courage in realizing that we are created in God's image. Is this a clue?

The book of Job contains a staggeringly poignant picture that doesn't answer my question rationally but is quite revealing: *Where were you when I laid the earth's foundation? Tell me, if you understand* —Job 38:4.

I don't understand. The book ends with a grand litany of God's works of creation and salvation—a mosaic of His character and divine essence.

In writing this little piece, I have come full circle again—back to the realization that my need to know God's origin is rooted in questions about my own origin. I really do want to know where He comes from. But, on this side of "glory," I will embrace and be at peace with what He *has* revealed to me. To know that He is God, that He is good, and that His steadfast love endures forever! *Soli Deo Gloria.*

What Is Unconditional Love?

Philip L. Kinley

*D*ear God, I thank You for Your mercy in giving me the incredible gift of your saving grace. I wholly accept Your sacrificial love for me. I believe it is unconditional; but what does it mean?

On the one hand, Your word assures that the one who believes in Jesus Christ will be saved (Acts 16:31). Is salvation limited only to believers in Christ? How do I answer my Asian friends who gladly accept God's love through Christ, yet question the fate of their parents or grandparents who never had the opportunity to hear and respond to the gospel's good news?

I believe You are at work even in places where the gospel has not yet been proclaimed and that Your saving love includes all who sincerely worship and honor the unknown. Your Word assures the times of ignorance God overlooked (Acts 17:30). Since the Creation Your invisible nature, power, and deity *have been clearly perceived in the things that have been made* —Romans 1:20 ESV. I believe Your love is for everyone and your will is the salvation of all persons (I Timothy 2:4). By faith, can I assure my friends their ancestors who worshiped an unknown God through ignorance will be saved?

Another question is, does Your judgement of sin contradict unconditional love? My understanding of unconditional love, *agape*, is that it is not limited by time, space, or the response of the object of love. If it is a love that "will not let me go," isn't it defeated if it is ultimately rejected by some and therefore is conditional upon acceptance?

I believe faith outruns reason and my belief in Your perfect goodness expressed in unconditional love cannot be defeated. Isn't Your love based on our freedom to accept it? Unfortunately, freedom of will has resulted in disobedience. All have sinned against You and Your love. Your solution to this dilemma is forgiveness through the atoning sacrifice of Your Son, Jesus Christ. Because the possibility of our salvation is made secure regardless of our choice, doesn't it become an unconditional benefit of the atonement? At the same time, Your holy love cannot allow sin to triumph. It must be judged and defeated by Your love. Ultimate love leaves the beloved free to choose one's own destiny.

God, is this the meaning of unconditional love?

Why Should I Pray?

Dale D. Landis

She was eleven years old and it was time for bed and prayers. But on this night she said, "Why should I pray? God doesn't answer me. Where is He? How do you know He is real? The only answer I could come up with was, "Just trust in Him, you will know." There were no theological answers for this moment. As a matter in fact it took me back to a time when I was about the same age when I asked the same questions. I remembered my dad reading Bible stories to my brother and me and helping us say our prayers, but I never saw or heard from God. Dad and Mom trusted in Him, so I did, too. And along the way I began to see glimpses of Him. I remember that night at youth camp when God revealed Himself to me and I began my walk with Him. The journey goes on and even today I find myself asking, "God, where are You? Reveal Yourself to me. I need to see You. I keep trusting and believing and realize I'm in good company because, Peter, who walked on the water with Jesus, later doubted and denied Him. And Jesus still asked him to be the leader of His church and to feed His sheep.

I love the way Peter teaches us to trust. He reminds us that trials will be part of our journey and that our faith will grow, and then he says, *You love him even though you have never seen him. Though you do not see him now, you trust him; and you rejoice with a glorious, inexpressible joy.* —1 Peter 1:8 NLT.

My eleven-year-old daughter grew up asking questions and still needs proof that God is real. She now asks her questions as she helps teach a women's Bible study. I watch her trust this unseen God in her job. I also know that her beautiful five-year-old son is going to ask questions about God, but for now his child-like faith is working, because he told Mommy that God lives in his heart.

I know that in a few short years he will say to his mom, "Why should I pray? God doesn't answer me. Where is He? How do you know He is real?" And she will say, "Just trust Him, you will know."

Thank you God, for honoring our search for You, for revealing Yourself to each of us in Your unique, mystical way. As we continue to doubt and wonder, allow Your Holy Spirit to surprise us with mini miracles of Your love.

Heaven for Me

Kerry B. Robinson

As a child my questions for God were multitude and mostly personal. Why did other children have four grandparents and I only had one? Would people at church treat me differently if I was not the pastor's son? What would our family be like if I had a sister instead of two brothers? How was it possible that my parents had lived before there was television??

Over the years my questions have changed significantly. These days my questions reflect my experiences in life. They are more inclusive of others and seem to have a focus beyond my personal needs. It is not that my personal questions have gone away rather it is that I have witnessed the needs of others. I have spent my adult life in pastoral ministry walking with people through the twists and turns of life. Young and old, rich and poor, formally educated and life educated, their experiences at the core of life are so similar that their questions carry the same sound. The more I hear them, the more I reframe my own questions. The more I reframe my questions, the more they become an affirmation rather than a question. The affirmation is simply amazement at the extent of God's grace in the lives of humanity.

Interestingly, my amazement at God's grace is not focused on His ability to extend mercy and forgiveness to the obvious "sinners" of the world. I can easily understand God's love and care for those caught in the broken places of life. Alcoholics, adulterers, liars, thieves, the abusively violent, and the multitude of those who demonstrate desperate need of healing and wholeness are obvious objects of grace. My amazement is in regard to God's grace extended to those who show no obvious need in their daily lives.

Those who hide their hurt in the pretense of religion are the source of my amazement. How can God be so patient with those who pretend they don't need Him? What tremendous love is His that He could love those who mock His grace through the arrogance of legalistic religion? Where does the grace to cover those who think they need no grace originate? This is truly the most amazing grace. This is authentic holiness. This is the love I long to celebrate for eternity. This is the relationship I was created to enjoy. To live in the presence of One who knows me and still loves me will be heaven to me.

A Purpose for Living

Harold A. Conrad

efore we question God, we must believe He exists, and I do with all my heart, soul, and mind. I also believe He is all-knowing (omniscient). He knows my past, present, and future, and He loves me.

In the light of these convictions, I'd like to ask Him, "Why did You let me live?" I was still-born. Seeing this, the doctor turned his attention to my mother, who immediately needed his assistance, before he cared for me. Seeing I was still lifeless when he came to me, he used his innovative ingenuity and gave me shock treatment, placing me quickly under cold running water and then warmer than normal water until I gasped for air, and by the will of God my heart began to beat.

I came into a dark world of financial depression, being one more mouth to feed, and body to clothe. Being reared by a sickly mother brought to my young life a great deal of insecurity and inward fear. At fourteen years of age I was called to the ministry and a few years later married a young lady who had been miraculously led to Christ sometime earlier, who also felt her call to Christian service. In our first pastorate and after eight years of marriage and the birth of three children, she developed a rapidly growing cancer of the colon and liver which took her life in three months. Nineteen faith warriors of the church had surrounded, anointed, and earnestly prayed for her healing, but none came.

Here I was a widower, less than thirty years of age, with three little ones. For four and a half years as a single parent, I attempted to raise the family. In 1960 I met a missionary to Africa, who was on furlough in the US, married her, enjoyed thirty-seven years of active and fruitful ministry in the church before she developed Alzheimer's disease. She recently passed away after twelve years of deterioration. Before her death all communication skills, except eye contact, were gone, her mobility, and her ability to care for herself. She was like a child one to two years of age. I ask, "What are You trying to teach me, Lord?" "What lessons do You want me to learn from this?" "Are You asking me to carry these crosses?" "Will my faithfulness in service to others today be eternally rewarded?" (2 Timothy 2:12) "Are there special assignments in life for certain individuals?" "Are the stronger asked to bear the burdens of the weaker?" I do believe You have a purpose for all You allow, a plan for each of our lives. You had such a plan for Your Son, for the Israelite slaves for four hundred years in Egypt, and I believe for a maiden woman I knew who cared for her mother until her mother died in her nineties. I believe as one of God's children, I must accept my past, present, and future as all springing from Your love.

How Can It Be?

Twila Tucker Briscoe

How awesome it is to know You love and indwell my heart and soul with Your grace and beauty. How can I ever know fully the brilliance of Your perpetual goodness which overflows in my soul every day of my life?

Almighty and everlasting God, could You ever allow a mere, mortal man to glimpse a single sight of Your hallowed face? I meditate on what it might be like to have been present on the hillside and to have listened as You taught Your children. I close my eyes and sense the velvet touch of Your loving hand as it reaches out to stroke the little ones.

And so, Lord, I would like to ask, just how did You create all the colors of the field, and the flowers of the world, and the music of the mountains that swells through the winds and creates the sound of wheels as it rifles through the trees?

All the beauty around me is consistent with the joy I experience when I think about Your love, Your creation, and Your patience with me. I need to know, Heavenly Father, how can I be at one with You and develop the virtues of temperance, self-control, diligence, strength of heart, contentment, and cheerfulness, that will keep me from being idle while I complete my journey on earth?

Oh, God, alert my senses to the glory all around me. I relish the scent of the chrysanthemums and study their perfect cut and gorgeous tones and I am propelled into a state of wonderment that drives me to shout, "How?" How could this be that they are so perfect, so flawless, and so desirable? The harmony and melody of nature is so perfect that I wish to ask again..."How?"

So, my precious Lord, can mortal mind ever comprehend the companionship You offer through the beauty of life and creation? Can mortal mind sequester a rigorous course of study that might lead to a path of heightened understanding and thereby attain a clearer view of Your magnificent masterpiece? How Can It Be? How, dear Father, can You love one who is so fallible? How can Your heart tolerate my inadequacies, my flawed sense of right, and my fledging perception of beauty?

I will wait, Father, wait on You and hold tightly to the dynamic of unconditional love manifested through the daily restoration of my soul when I gaze upon Your face. But my heart will cry out... "How? How can this be?"

Is Suicide Forgiven?

Charles N. Moore

The physicians had tried about ten drugs. Each one seemed to set me on fire more that the previous one. The pain was unbearable. The side effects included strong desires to commit suicide. I was in the hospital eleven days. Two months later I was in for eight days. One sympathetic physician said, "You poor man." I hung on to my faith in Christ. Then I lost all hope of recovery four times.

After three months, my wife, Elizabeth, and my daughter consulted an excellent pharmacist. He said, "Get him off all of the drugs as fast as you can." Elizabeth began cutting doses in half, then one fourth. After some time, I had practically no dizziness, nausea, headache, or terrible burning pain. I could read a bill and understand it.

During the three months of *fire*, I memorized scriptures and songs. I sang *I Am the Lord's* and *Wonderful Peace* repeatedly.

Jesus' promise concerning His peace helped some. But I continued to ask God, "Will You forgive me if I commit suicide?"

One day I found a small booklet by Joyce Meyers entitled *Peace*. She wrote something about not expecting God to give you peace mainly on the emotional level. I have had three experiences of God's peace on the emotional level. I realize I was trying to duplicate this *emotional* experience.

She said, "If you sincerely asked the Lord for His peace, you already have it. However you must appropriate it and activate it." I immediately remembered preaching this advice.

When I began to accept this fact and began *calmly* and *peacefully* facing each moment of life in this manner, the *fire* inside and outside began to subside. I made David's words my own. When being chased by Saul, he said, *I will not die but live, and will proclaim what the LORD has done* —Psalm 118:17.

My attitude changed. When I hear about one of God's children committing suicide, I am quick to remember my impossible experience. I do not judge the person involved. I now realize that while I was under the influence of many drugs, my ability to think was greatly impaired.

Would God have forgiven me? I like to think that He would. But He *answered* in ways far beyond the question. How? All of life is so very special now. My loved ones, my church, my wife, and my children stand out in bold relief. Never has love and life been so exceedingly meaningful, precious, and sacred.

The Origins of Our Questions

Ronald V. Duncan

"Why can't we eat from that tree?" Perhaps a question pondered by Adam and Eve.

It seems to me that most if not all our questions of God or about God emerge out of two origins: the rejection of the sovereignty of God and the exercise of our free will. There are answers to many difficult questions found within the Scriptures. But as is the case with some questions, when one is answered, two or three more emerge. For instance, to understand life and death from the sovereignty of God point of view, one could state, *The LORD gave, and the LORD has taken away; blessed be the name of the LORD* —Job 1:21 ESV. On a certain level you have answered the question of why some die "before their time" and others do not. Yet when death occurs from a tragic automobile accident caused by a tire blow out or an intoxicated driver, then the exercise of our free will to question asks: why did God let this happen? Or was this the will of God? So we see that acceptance on one level may lead to more difficult questions on another level. The problem is the believer must exercise regularly the higher belief in the sovereignty of God. If our logic fails us, then by faith, we must acknowledge and truly accept the sovereignty of God.

This causes the American Christian who is accustomed to the exercise of the free will not only in faith issues, but government issues to cringe and assert inalienable rights. So within the heart and mind, the cognitive dissonance between these two ideas begin battle. Are these two ideas equal? Does one take precedence over the other? What happens when they are in conflict? It seems to me that the sovereignty of God must take precedence and the believer by faith accepts what cannot be answered or solved.

I further contend that many of our so called "unanswerable questions" are answered within Scriptures. The problem is not the question or the answer, but the ability of the questioner to engage Scripture correctly and thoroughly. The American Christian believer today has a very shallow knowledge and less of an understanding of the knowledge he or she possesses of Scripture. A surface understanding and knowledge of Scripture is essential if we are to engage in fruitful understanding of difficult questions.

The question I would then have for God if given my audience would be why did you provide for your creation, free will? It has caused so much pain in the world since the beginning.

Biographies

John L. Albright and his wife, Ruth, live in Alexandria, Indiana. He has served churches in Ohio, Indiana, Illinois, and Michigan and for fourteen years was youth director for the National Board of Christian Education of the Church of God. *(see page 139)*

Donald L. Allbaugh is a forensic therapist who provides treatment to a court-mandated population of sexual abusers. Don received his baccalaureate degree from Taylor University, a Master of Social Work from Indiana University and a Master of Theological Studies from Anderson University School of Theology. He and his wife, Connie, have four adult children. *(see page 123)*

Norma Massie Armogum has been a storyteller since childhood but has only recently begun submitting her work for publication. Norma has a BA from Anderson University. She is director of administrative services for WQME, a contemporary Christian radio station, and Covenant Productions, a video production company. Norma enjoys living near her two sons, daughter-in-law, and three grandchildren, gardening, and being involved in the prayer ministry at her church. *(see page 121)*

James H. Bailey has a regular column in the Anderson, Indiana, newspaper, *The Herald Bulletin*. He and his wife, Bonnie, live in Anderson, Indiana, and are the parents of four adult daughters. *(see page 71)*

Lolly Bargerstock-Oyler and her husband, Tim, live in Anderson, Indiana, and are the parents of two sons. Lolly practiced as a clinical social worker for fifteen years before taking her current position as assistant professor of social work at Anderson University. *(see page 105)*

Cheryl Johnson Barton and her husband, Bernie, have served as Church of God missionaries in Japan for thirty years. They are parents of two adult children and have two grandchildren. Cheryl is a 1976 graduate of Anderson University and was ordained to ministry in 2001. *(see page 29)*

Norman E. Beard and his wife, Louetta, live in Anderson, Indiana. After forty-three years at Anderson University, he retired as Dean of International Education Emeritus. He has provided leadership for the World Conference of the Church of God and the American Red Cross at the local, state, and national levels. *(see page 135)*

Donald G. Boggs is an Emmy awarded producer. He is director and chair of Communications and Theatre Arts at Anderson University. Don also serves as general manager for the University's radio and television department, WQME and Covenant Productions. A recent production, *A Ripple of Hope,* has bought national attention to the 1968 speech of Robert Kennedy announcing the assassination of Martin Luther King Jr. Don and his wife, Tamara, have three children. *(see page 27)*

Twila Tucker Briscoe is the owner and administrator of Alpha Christian Child Care Center. Twila earned her BA from Anderson University and continued her education at Wichita State University and Radford University. She and her husband, Charles, have two adult children and five grandchildren. *(see page 171)*

Sam Bruce was president of Wesley College in Florence, Mississippi. He is a pastor and an instructor at Mid-America Christian University. Sam earned his Master of Divinity degree from Anderson University School of Theology and his Doctor of Ministry from Fuller Theology Seminary. He and his wife, Sandie, have two daughters. *(see page 115)*

Kathleen Davey Buehler is a preacher's kid who has spent more than thirty years in the national publishing ministry of the Church of God. One of her passions is teaching children about the Bible and its Author. *(see page 117)*

Barry L. Callen is the editor of Anderson University Press and the author of over thirty books. He is the former dean of both Anderson University and Anderson University School of Theology. Barry and his wife, Jan, live in Anderson, Indiana. *(see page 17)*

Jan Slattery Callen and her husband, Barry, live in Anderson, Indiana. Jan is a high school English teacher. She and Barry each have a grown son and are the grandparents of six. *(see page 109)*

Dondeena Fleenor Caldwell and her husband, Maurice, live in Anderson, Indiana. They were career missionaries in Mexico and Brazil. Dondeena was editor of *Missions* magazine for over sixteen years and is the author of the book *Amazon Adventures*. *(see page 113)*

Frederick D. Clemens has served as a United Methodist minister for over twenty years in Virginia and Alabama. Fred and his wife, Becky, live in Huntsville, Alabama, where he serves as pastor and chaplain for Crestwood Medical Center. *(see page 79)*

Sam Collins has written for Church of God publications for more than thirty years. A graduate of Anderson University and its School of Theology, he currently edits adult Sunday school curriculum and *Pathways to God* magazine. Sam and his wife, Sharon, have two sons. *(see page 75)*

Harold A. Conrad served the Church of God for fifty-six years, twenty-two years as a pastor, twenty years as a church pensions executive, and fourteen years as a consultant. He was married to Naomi and is the father of four. Harold is a graduate of Anderson University, Christian Theology Seminary, and has a Doctor of Divinity degree from Mid-America Christian University. *(see page 169)*

Sara Cook and her husband, Mark McCleary, live in Belfast, Northern Ireland. Currently she serves as Director of Family and Community at the East Belfast Mission where she does community development and reconciliation work. She earned her BA degree in social work and history from Anderson University and her MA degree in social work from Boston University. *(see page 25)*

C. Richard Craghead has retired from teaching and administration at Warner Pacific College. He was youth editor for Warner Press and was an associate pastor in Sacramento, California. Richard holds a BA and BTh from WPC, an MDiv from Anderson University School of Theology and a DMin from San Francisco Theological Seminary. Richard and his wife, Ardys, have two children. He writes adult curriculum for Church of God Ministries. *(see page 31)*

Kenneth E. Crouch and his wife, Carolyn, live in Billings, Montana. Ken is a minister in the United Church of Christ serving the Mayflower congregation in Billings. Active in theater, he also has been on a mission trip to Nicaragua and participates in the Safe School Coalition. *(see page 55)*

Mort Crim is a retired television and radio journalist. He was a New York based correspondent with ABC for five years and for more than thirty-five years anchored the news for television stations in Detroit, Philadelphia, and Chicago. His *Second Thoughts* radio feature was syndicated on more than 1300 stations. Mort is the author of seven inspirational books. He and his wife, Irene, live in Jacksonville, Florida. *(see pages 6 and 19)*

Doris Aldridge Dale's journey has afforded her the privilege of being a pastor's wife, mother of four, and grandmother of ten. She served in the role of national coordinator for Women of the Church of God and national coordinator for Church of God Global Missions. *(see page 33)*

Milian B. Dekich is pastor of Fairview Church of God in Falkville, Alabama. He and his wife, Barbara, have two children who both attend Auburn University. Astronomy is one of Milan's hobbies. *(see page 47)*

Ronald V. Duncan and his wife, Martha, live in Anderson, Indiana. Ron has pastored in Ohio, Indiana, and Texas. He is the general director of Church of God Ministries and a retired chaplain in the Army National Guard with the rank of colonel. *(see pages 5 and 175)*

Jerry Eddy is a graduate of Anderson University and its School of Theology. He is married to Julie, and has a daughter. Jerry has worked with the American Friends Service Committee, the social action arm of the Society of Friends, and currently teaches real estate finance and student success courses at Sinclair Community College. Leading workshops on community involvement and conflict resolution has nourished his spiritual journey. *(see page 35)*

Arthur R. Eikamp was born and grew up in Gary, South Dakota, during the dust storms of the Great Depression. He graduated from Anderson University in Anderson, Indiana, and Yale Divinity School. Arthur and his wife, Norma, spent two years ministering to agricultural migrants from the Rio Grande to the Mexican border before spending thirty-five years as missionaries in Japan where he was honored by the Emperor. They have now retired to the woods along the Oregon coast. *(see page 83)*

Raymond A. Freer is an 1965 Anderson University graduate and after receiving his masters degree began teaching at his alma mater. For twelve years he was department chair. Ray retired in 2009 and now serves as an event coordinator for the Anderson Center for the Arts. *(see page 87)*

Mick Gilliam has served congregations in Oregon, Florida, Ohio, and Indiana, and has also taught in Christian colleges and seminaries. He and his wife, Linda, have two children. Mick enjoys spending time with his family, participating in outdoor activities, playing racquetball, performing jazz, songwriting, and cycling. Recently Mick received a Doctor of Worship Studies. Linda works is a copyright agent for Gaither Music Company. *(see page 161)*

Thomas R. Harbron is a native of Clinton, Iowa, where he graduated from high school. He attended Anderson University before earning a degree in electrical engineering from Iowa State University. For thirty-eight years he taught physics, mathematics, and computer science at Anderson University. Tom and his wife, Jean, live in Anderson, Indiana, and are the parents of three adult children and grandparents of two. *(see page 23)*

Doug Hall is publications director for Physicians Committee for Responsible Medicine and the author of six cartoon books, including *Less Than Entirely Sanctified* and *Reborn to Be Wild*. He graduated from Anderson University in 1978. Doug currently lives in Anderson, Indiana, with his wife, Marla. They have three children, two dogs, and a cat who refuses to reveal her identity. *(see page 39)*

Kenneth F. Hall and his wife, Arlene, live in Anderson, Indiana. Ken was an editor of curriculum at Warner Press and a former professor of Christian education at Anderson University. He has authored several books. *(see page 157)*

Daniel C. Harman and his wife, Betty Ann, live in Anderson, Indiana. Dan was a Church of God pastor for more than forty years, serving in Indiana, Illinois, Tennessee, Kentucky, and California. For nine years he was book editor at Warner Press. Dan has authored four books and nearly 2000 articles for more than 200 publications. *(see page 119)*

Sharon Cook Harrison is a seminar speaker, interior decorator, wedding and special events consultant/coordinator, and a certified judge for the *Miss America* system. Her message is dynamic, inspiring, and redemptive, as she speaks from the heart to women who have experienced incredible challenges and astonishing breakthroughs, with a witty and insightful delivery of hope and inspiration. www.sharonjcook.com *(see page 159)*

Stephen Hill is a gospel singer who is concentrating on his solo ministry. As a backup singer, his credits include Dolly Parton, Don McLean, Jake Hess, and Marie Osmond. Stephen and his wife, Kathy, have three children. *(see page 15)*

Barry F. Hoffman *(1942-2010)* was most recently a counselor serving sixteen years before retiring in 2007. He served eleven years as an editor for Warner Press. Barry earned his undergraduate degree from Findley College in Ohio and a graduate degree from Christian Theological Seminary in Indianapolis. With his wife of forty-five years, Nancy, he has three children. *(see page 91)*

Laura Withrow Hoak served for many years with her late husband, Oral, in pastoral ministry. She is a writer of church curriculum and the author of several books. Laura and her husband, Duane, live in Anderson, Indiana. *(see page 73)*

Donald D. Johnson was a missionary to Guyana, South America, and Trinidad, West Indies. He pastored in Atwater, California, and Anderson, Indiana. Don was a seminary professor at Anderson University School of Theology and an administrator with the Missionary Board of the Church of God. He and his wife, Betty Jo, have three children, all of whom are presently or have been missionaries. *(see page 111)*

Don Deena Johnson serves the Church of God as a missionary in Japan. Her area of responsibility is discipleship, Christian education, and leadership training. *(see page 41)*

John M. Johnson and his wife, Gwen, have served as missionaries with the Church of God in South Korea, Egypt, and Lebanon, where John was president of Mediterranean Bible College and pastor of Beirut International Church. The Johnsons live in Portland, Oregon, where they are involved in training future missionaries and mission-minded pastors at Warner Pacific College. *(see page 131)*

Phil L. Kinley graduated from Anderson College and its School of Theology, and has advanced degrees in education and missiology. Phil and his wife, Phyllis, were missionaries in Japan for over forty years where he planted and pastored churches, taught seminary students, and was principal of a junior-senior high school. The Kinleys now live in Anderson, Indiana. *(see page 163)*

Phyllis Gillespie Kinley spent forty-three years as a missionary in Japan. Involved in contemplative/meditative prayer for over forty years, she ministers to a contemplative prayer group that meets in her home. She and her husband are also deeply interested in cross-cultural relationships and experiences. *(see page 49)*

Dale D. Landis retired in 2010 as worship pastor from South Meridian Church of God in Anderson, Indiana. Dale and his wife, Bonnie, have two children and live in Pendleton, Indiana. He earned his undergraduate degree from Anderson University. *(see page 165)*

David L. Lawson is a retired minister with most of his service being in national ministry with the Church of God. He served as staff member in World Service for twenty-eight years, the last nine as executive director. He then served as associate executive secretary of the Leadership Council for eight years before his retirement in 1997. David earned his BS degree from Anderson University and MA from Ball State University. He was honored with a DD from Mid-America Christian University. *(see page 141)*

Juanita Evans Leonard is associate professor emeritus at Anderson University School of Theology and a licensed marriage and family therapist. Juanita is a widely published author. She resides in South Carolina. *(see page 69)*

Alvin Lewis and his wife Juanita live in Jackson, Mississippi. Al earned his PhD from Kansas State University and has served as a pastor in Wisconsin, Kansas, and Mississippi. He was National Director of Adult and Family Life Education/Leadership Development for the Board of Christian Education of the Church of God. He has also served with the National Association. *(see page 137)*

Jeffery K. Lockhart and his wife, Nancy are the parents of three grown children. Jeff earned his undergraduate degree from Anderson University, majoring in accounting and management. He has provided for his family as a commercial real estate banker. *(see page 143)*

Jim B. Luttrell has served as minister of Christian education, youth, and Christian growth in Tennessee, Ohio, Indiana, Wisconsin and was senior pastor in Michigan, Missouri, and Alabama. Jim received the Distinguished Ministries Award from the Anderson University School of Theology. He is minister of music in Canton, Georgia, where he lives with his wife, Wendy. *(see page 103)*

Jim Lyon and his wife Maureen live in Anderson, Indiana. Jim is the senior pastor of Madison Park Church of God and speaker for *ViewPoint*, the CBH-English radio broadcast for Mass Media. *(see page 43)*

Jeanette Morehead MacMillian is married to a Nazarene pastor and they are the parents of three children. Jeanette earned her undergraduate degree in English from Eastern Nazarene College. She has been published in *Cup of Comfort for Mothers and Daughters*. *(see page 101)*

David E. Markle and his wife Peggy have served the Church of God in North Carolina, Michigan, Indiana, and Oregon. Dr. Markle is senior pastor at Park Place Church of God, Anderson, Indiana. *(see page 147)*

Deborah Zarka Miller and her husband, Jerry, live in Anderson, Indiana. She teaches creative writing at Anderson University and speaks frequently to church groups and professional organizations in central Indiana. Her current writing projects include a young adult novel, *A Star for Robbins Chapel*, picture book texts, and personal essays. *(see page 37)*

Charles N. Moore *(1930-2009)* pastored five churches. He was married to Elizabeth Germany Moore for over fifty-five years. They have adult three children. Charles earned a masters degree from the Anderson University School of Theology. *(see page 173)*

Leslie H. Mosier is a retired chaplain in the US Air Force. As a member of the editorial department of Warner Press while in seminary, Les wrote for and edited *Vital Christianity*, as well as curriculum. He and his wife, Joyce, live in Franklin, Tennessee. Les and Joyce are the parents of an adult son and have two grandsons. *(see page 125)*

Judy Spencer Nelon serves on the board of directors for both the Gospel Music Association and the Southern Gospel Music Association. She has been the vice-president of Manna Music which owns such songs as "Sweet, Sweet Spirit," "Through It All," and "How Great Thou Art." www.judynelon.com *(see page 133)*

Gene W. Newberry *(1915-2009)* was a former dean of Anderson University School of Theology. He has authored four books. Gene and his wife, Agnes, were the parents of three daughters. They had one granddaughter and a great-grandson. *(see page 67)*

Helen Jones Newell and her husband, Arlo, live in Anderson, Indiana. She taught in the Bible and Religion department at Anderson University and has written adult curriculum for Warner Press. *(see page 65)*

Richard H. Petersen and his wife, Barbara, live in Scarborough, Maine. Now retired, Dick was the founding senior pastor of Christchurch of Portland, Maine. He was the executive director of the Bible Society of Maine, working in cooperation with the International and American Bible Society. *(see page 63)*

D. Dewayne Repass serves as chief development officer for Church of God Ministries in Anderson, Indiana. He is a graduate of Mid-America Christian University. Dewayne and his wife, Brenda, had pastorates in Missouri, Ohio, Louisiana, Oklahoma, Florida, and Indiana. Dewayne was associate state minister for Indiana Ministries. *(see page 151)*

Imy Tate Rhule is Assistant Professor of English Emerita from Anderson University where she taught for twenty years. Imy also taught English at Pendleton Heights High School for thirteen years. Imy earned her BA from Anderson University and MA from Ball State University. She and her husband Dwayne are the parents of four children. *(see page 45)*

Kerry B. Robinson has been senior pastor of East Side Church of God in Anderson, Indiana, since 1996. As the primary voice of this missional congregation, he speaks weekly to people of various ages who are discovering the hope of Jesus Christ in their lives. Kerry and his wife, Becky, are the parents of two adult sons. *(see page 167)*

Joy May Sherman is the community connection pastor at Maiden Lane Church of God in Springfield, Ohio. She is a 2003 graduate of the Anderson University School of Theology and a lover of God's Word. Joy is married to Steve and is a mom to Elijah Hunter. Joy and her family enjoy camping, hiking, playing games, and discovering what new things God has in store for them. *(see page 61)*

Fred H. Shively has combined the careers of being a pastor with teaching and introducing students to ministry in the world. For over thirty years he has been on the faculty of Anderson University and travels with students around the world. He is married to Kay, who also teaches at the university. They are the parents of two adult sons. *(see page 145)*

Kay Murphy Shively is a wife, mother, and grandmother and holds bachelor's and master's degrees in English. Though retired, she teaches freshman writing part time at Anderson University. Kay and her husband, Fred, reside in Anderson, Indiana. *(see page 97)*

David C. Shultz has ministered in the Church of God since 1967, most of those years as a pastor. The son of missionaries to the West Indies, he is married to Karon, who herself grew up in the home of veteran Church of God pastors. David and Karon are the parents of three grown children and have eight grandchildren. *(see page 59)*

Risë Wood Singer enjoys writing and singing. Recently she realized a lifetime dream when she recorded her first CD, *Risë Sings Her Favorites*. Since then she has performed several concerts and is enjoying her singing career. DRBsinger@aol.com *(see page 85)*

Margaret Jones Smith lives in Penney Farms, Florida. She is a former editor of Church of God *Missions* magazine and also edited the books wirtten by her late husband, John W. V. Smith. Margaret and John are the parents of three sons. *(see page 93)*

James L. Sparks and his wife, Susan, live in Battle Creek, Michigan. They have one daughter and three grandchildren. James is the senior pastor of North Avenue Church of God. He has written for several religious and secular publications. *(see page 95)*

William P. Soetenga and his wife, Janet, have four adult children and six grandchildren. Bill is a Warner Pacific and Anderson School of Theology graduate. After pastoral service in Marion, South Dakota, and Madison, Wisconsin, he retired in 2003 as Pastor Emeritus from West Anderson Church of God in Anderson, Indiana. *(see page 107)*

Norman W. Steinaker has been an educator for more than fifty-six years. He has taught all ages from pre-school to doctoral candidates. Norm has had five books published, and is working on three more. He teaches both online and on site. Norm and his wife, Blanche, have two children and two grandchildren. There are four "Fs" that he lives by—faith, family, friends, and fellowship. Life is good and the future is bright. *(see page 51)*

Christie Smith Stephens and her husband, Stan, live in Anderson, Indiana. Christie is a writer and an advocate for survivors of domestic and sexual abuse/violence. She is the cofounder of a social service agency in Anderson. With David Liverett she collaborated on the book, *Oh, to be in Miss Collier's class again!* *(see page 4)*

Christa Sterken is a freelance writer who strives to encourage people to embrace the day. She feels deep gratitude for the lessons in her life, for her beloved family and especially for a faith that sustains. *(see page 77)*

Charles R. Shumate is president of Church Builders Plus. He received his EdD in educational leadership from Ball State University and is the author of four books. Charles and his wife Laretta have two daughters and five grandchildren. He is an avid sportsman and pilot. He finds great fulfillment in playing with his grandchildren in their tree house. *(see page 149)*

Linda Elmore Teeple is a wife, mother, grandmother, licensed marriage and family therapist, dog lover, and writer. She resides in Anderson, Indiana, with her husband, Rex. She earned a masters degree from Indiana University and is a graduate of the Indianapolis Gestalt Institute. *(see page 53)*

Barbara Clausen Theodore lives with her husband, Lee, in California. She is retired from Whirlpool Corporation in Benton Harbor, Michigan, where she was part of a management team working in market research as a qualitative research analyst. Barbara attended Anderson College and business and management courses at Whirlpool Corporation. In her first marriage to Paul Clausen, she had two children. *(see page 21)*

Donna S. Thomas, cofounder and leader of a creative ministry in missions venture, is also an author, speaker, and consultant. She and her husband, Chuck, graduated from Anderson College, planted a church in Wichita, Kansas, and parented three sons. Donna now has thirteen grandchildren. Her ministry has taken her to seventy-nine countries, many times developing and leading national leaders in building the kingdom of God in their sphere of influence. *(see page 57)*

J. Paul Vincent has served in the English Department of Asbury University since 1976. He holds a PhD in American literature from Syracuse University. He is currently working on a short devotional volume on the "rest of faith" as articulated by writers of the nineteenth-century holiness revival. Paul and his wife, Anne, have one son and live in Lexington, Kentucky. *(see page 99)*

William A. White and his wife, Pam, live in Anderson, Indiana. Bill is a retired adult editor of BRIDGES curriculum. He is the father of four grown children. *(see page 153)*

Jack W. Williams has served his country as journalist, columnist, diarist, satirist, blogger, publications director, magazine editor, communications lecturer, editorial consultant, ad man, after-dinner speaker, and all around poor wayfaring stranger. He is working on his memoir, *My Life as a Man.* Jack and his wife, Karen, have one son. *(see page 127)*

Nathan J. Willowby and his wife Jill live in Milwaukee, Wisconsin. Nathan received a BA from Anderson University in 2005, a MDiv from Duke Divinity School in 2008, and is currently working toward a PhD in Systematic Theology and Theological Ethics at Marquette University. He also presently serves as interim pastor at Crossroads Church of God in Milwaukee. *(see page 155)*

Richard L. Willowby lives in Anderson, Indiana, with his wife, Cheryl. He is the pastor of Hope Community Church of God in Clarksville, Indiana. Rich and Cheryl are the parents of three adult children. *(see page 129)*

Kathryn Womack-States lives in Anderson, Indiana, with her husband, Tim. Kathryn and Tim are the parents of twins. For the past seventeen years, Kathryn has worked as a school social worker. *(see page 81)*

Carma Withrow Wood is associate pastor of worship arts at Park Place Church of God in Anderson, Indiana. She was co-founder and for sixteen years was worship arts director and pastor at Mountain Park Community Church in Phoenix, Arizona. Carma has a BA and an Associate Degree from Anderson University. She and her husband, Randy Hammel, live in Alexandria, Indiana. Carma is the mother of three adult children and has one granddaughter. *(see page 89)*

Acknowledgements

This book would never have been finished if my wife, Avis, had not taken a large role in the editing and in the care she has given me.

My illness has slowed the process of drawing, but my writer friends have once more contributed many wonderful stories. I thank you.

Tammy Burrell, who has been my assistant since 1988, once again has used her skills in helping with the layout of this book.

Many thanks to Arthur Kelly for his endorsement and editorial assistance.

Thanks to Charles Shumate for his suggestions in making the book more user friendly.

My thanks to Michelangelo for his fresco of *Creation of Man* in the Sistine Chapel, used on the cover.

Keep asking, and it will be given to you.

–Matthew 7:7 ISV

Thoughts for Small Group Gatherings

1. Gather a group that can commit to one hour a week for four to six weeks. A group reflecting a diversity of viewpoints provides a stimulating variety of both spiritual experience and understanding.

2. Choose three or four stories from the *Questions for God* book that are of interest to the group to discuss.

3. Here are some questions that are pertinent to ask during the group session:

- What is the story or writer saying about God?

- Does the story bring new insight, observation, or understanding to your spiritual journey? Each story can bring renewed insight or new light as never seen before.

- Spiritual journeys have growth opportunities as we search for fuller understanding. Are there any of the writings that are closely related to your own experience? How?

- What are the implications of these writings for personal spiritual growth?

- If you could personally ask God one question, what would you ask?

The study of this book should be considered a continuing process. Understanding always has an open end to the life-long learner. Treat it as a continual dialogue between these stories and your story.

Books by David Liverett

When Hope Shines Through
This 240 page book has 110 lighthouse drawings and 106 essays from 90 different writers.

Faith for the Journey
This 304 page book is an inspirational paperback with 100 church drawings and 103 essays from 98 different writers.

Love, Bridges of Reconciliation
This 176 page book has 67 bridge drawings and 72 essays from 68 writers.

Oh, to be in Miss Collier's class again!
This 192 page book is a paperback of poetry and stories about growing up in Austinville, Alabama, in 1950. Written by Christie Smith Stephens and illustrated by David Liverett.

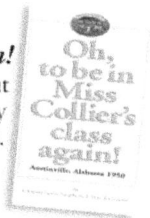

This Is My Story
146 of the World's Greatest Gospel Singers
This 297 page book, published by Thomas Nelson, features biographies and pen-and-ink drawings of 146 gospel music singers.

Just Beyond the Passage
Life's Changes in art and Story
This 144 page book is an inspirational paperback with 60 door, gate, and arch drawings and 60 essays from different writers.

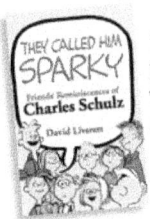

They Called Him Sparky:
Friends' Reminiscences of Charles Schulz
This 112 page book contains stories about Schulz's life from his early years in St. Paul, Minnesota. Features several of his *Young Pillars* cartoons.

Those Grand Ole Country Music Stars
This 248 page book features biographies and pen-and-ink drawings of 217 country music personalities.

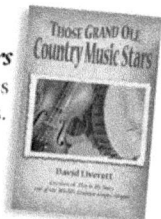

Available online, or ask for them where you bought this book.